McCARTHY
ZEROS
IN!

Here Senator Eugene McCarthy spells out, in words that leave no doubt about his meaning, his position on the most burning problems America faces in the world today.

Here is McCarthy on Vietnam. On China. On Europe. On the arms race. On America's past mistakes and future options. And the many other vital issues long in need of clear thinking and plain talking.

Here is the rare combination of wit, knowledge, razor-edged intelligence, and absolute refusal to mouth the old, tired clichés that has made Eugene McCarthy the most amazing and exciting figure in perhaps the most fateful election year in our country's history.

Eugene McCarthy

The
Limits
of
Power

AMERICA'S ROLE IN THE WORLD

Senator Eugene J. McCarthy

A DELL BOOK

To Ellen McCarthy and Mary McCarthy

Published by
DELL PUBLISHING CO., INC.
750 Third Avenue
New York, N.Y. 10017
Dell ® TM 681510, Dell Publishing Co., Inc.
Reprinted by arrangement with
Holt, Rinehart and Winston, Inc.
New York, N.Y.
Printed in U.S.A.
First Dell edition—April 1968

Introduction

Since the original publication of this book in 1967, the war in Vietnam has become a more "dubious battle" and the evidence of national crisis in other areas has become much clearer.

In 1963 America was characterized by a spirit of confidence and of hope, of openness to the future and of enthusiasm. There were good reasons for these attitudes. For the first time in our history, it appeared certain that with careful direction the economy of this country could be made more and more productive, that it has the potential of meeting the needs of all Americans as well as of supplying material help to the underdeveloped nations of the world.

Our reputation abroad had reached a postwar high and the fear that America might turn away from its responsibilities after the war had been dispelled by the clear evidence that we were prepared to respond to the new demands of world leadership. In Western Europe particularly, nations welcomed President Kennedy and his family with great enthusiasm whenever they visited the Continent. The other countries of the world—particularly in Latin America—had great confidence in the promise of the Alliance for Progress. Our own young people in the Peace Corps were an inspiration to the world.

Today we find an altogether different response, both at home and abroad. It is difficult to find a world capital which the President of the United States can visit in reasonable safety and security. Latin Americans are disillusioned, not over the total failure of the Alliance for Progress, but because it has fallen so far short of its potential and its goal. The war in Vietnam does not have the respect or the support of our traditional allies—those nations which we have counted as holding a decent opinion on world policy.

At home, we are not moving toward a Great Society, but rather we are a Stalled Society.

We are engaging in a war of questionable legality and questionable constitutionality:

• a war which is diplomatically indefensible. It is the first war in this century in which the United States finds itself without the support of the decent opinion of mankind.

• a war which cannot be defended in the context of our own judgment of history, but can only be presented as an extension of the judgment of an era which is now passed. What is necessary is a realization that the United States is a part of the movement of history itself; that it cannot stand apart, attempting to control the world by imposing covenants and treaties and by violent military intervention; that our role is not to police the planet, but to use military strength with restraint and within limits while at the same time we make available to the world the great power of our economy, of our knowledge, and of our goodwill.

• a war which is not defensible even in military terms, which runs contrary to the advice of our greatest generals—Ridgway, Shoup, Gavin and MacArthur —all of whom admonished us against becoming involved in a land war in Asia. Estimate after estimate as to the time and the military commitment necessary for victory have had to be revised upward—always upward; more troops, more extensive bombing and a widening and intensification of the war. Projection after projection of success has been proved wrong.

With the escalation of our military commitment has come a parallel overleaping of objectives: from protecting South Vietnam, to nation-building in South Vietnam, to protecting all of Southeast Asia, and ultimately to suggesting that the safety and security of the United States itself is at stake in Asia.

Finally, it is a war which is morally wrong. Official statements of objectives cannot be accepted as an honest judgment of why we are in Vietnam. It has become increasingly difficult to justify the methods and the instruments of war we are using, as we have moved from limited target and restricted weapons to greater variety and more destructive instruments of war, and as we have extended the area of operations to the heart of North Vietnam.

The war cannot stand the test of proportion and of prudent judgment. It is no longer possible to prove that the good that may come with what is called "victory" is proportionate to the loss of life and property and to the other disorders that follow from that war.

Let me summarize the cost of the war up to this point:

• the physical destruction of a small, weak nation by the military operation of the most powerful nation on this earth;

• 100,000 to 150,000 civilian casualties in South Vietnam alone, according to estimates made *prior* to the recent Tet offensive which was so costly to both sides;

• the uprooting and fracturing of the social structure of South Vietnam, where one-fourth to one-third of the population are now refugees;

• for the United States, over 20,000 combat dead and some 120,000 wounded—a casualty total that surpasses that of the Korean War.

• a monthly expenditure on the war by the United States of 2 to 3 billion dollars.

I am also concerned over the bearing of the war on other areas of United States responsibility:

• the failure to appropriate adequate funds for the poverty program, for housing, for education and other national needs, and the prospect of additional cuts;

• the drastic reduction of our foreign-aid program in other parts of the world;

• the dangerous rise of inflation and, as an indirect but serious consequence, the devaluation of the British pound;

• the international monetary crisis with the entire world monetary system threatened by lack of confidence in the dollar.

The issue of the war in Vietnam is not a separate issue but is one which must be dealt with in relation to other problems—that is the context in which I decided, late in 1967, to take the case to the people of the United States by entering Presidential primaries. I was hopeful that a challenge might alleviate the sense of political helplessness and restore to many people a belief in the processes of American politics and of American government. I think the challenge has had that effect.

I am not for peace at any price, but for an honorable, rational, and political solution to this war, a solution which I believe will enhance our world position, encourage the respect of our adversaries, permit us to give the necessary attention to our other commitments abroad—both military and nonmilitary—and leave us with the resources and moral energy to deal effectively with the pressing domestic problems of the United States itself.

EUGENE J. McCARTHY

March 1968

Preface

If this book has a principal theme, it is that our foreign policy should be more restrained and, insofar as prudent judgment can determine, more closely in keeping with the movement of history. If it has a personal mark, it is that which I believe Adlai Stevenson would have made on American foreign policy, had his ideas and his attitudes been translated into political reality.

Its general practical conclusions are: first, that the United States should be more ready than it has in the past to use international or multi-national agencies so as to show more certainly our "decent respect to the opinions of mankind"; second, that our use of instrumentalities and devices such as the Central Intelligence Agency and of military influence established through the distribution and sale of arms should be restricted and more carefully controlled; and third, that the Senate, principally through the Foreign Relations Committee, should more competently, conscientiously, and effectively exercise its constitutional responsibility in the formulation and conduct of the foreign policy of the United States.

For assistance in preparing this book for publication I am especially indebted to Louise FitzSimons of my office and to members of the staff of the Foreign Relations Committee.

EUGENE J. MCCARTHY

June 1967

Contents

	Introduction	5
	Preface	11
1	Time for a Fresh Look	17
2	Power Through People	23
3	Power Through Gunpowder	37
4	Power Through Pawns	69
5	Rhetoric or Reality in Latin America	95
6	Conflicts or Cooperation in Europe	115
7	Africa and the Middle East: Patience Pays	125
8	Micronesia: Our Trust	137
9	Vietnam: In Dubious Battle	147
10	China: Need We Collide?	155
	INDEX	183

The
Limits
of
Power

1
Time for
a Fresh Look

United States foreign policy until the Eisenhower years in the White House was relatively clear, direct, and limited. In the nineteenth century, we were a developing nation, concerned primarily with domestic expansion. As to the outside world, we still followed George Washington's recommendations against involvement in foreign affairs, and we repeatedly restated the Monroe Doctrine as a warning to any nation that might be tempted to interfere in our affairs or in the affairs of other nations in the Western hemisphere.

We did, however, extend our interests west across the Pacific, reaching out to China and Japan. In the Far East we insisted, first, on the open-door policy to insure trade opportunity for Americans and, later, on a most-favored-nation policy to prevent any other nation's being given concessions that were not also given to us.

The Spanish American War was a venture inconsistent with our past—that is, the past of the nineteenth century—and with any policy previously recognized or stated.

In 1917, we entered World War I in order to preserve Western civilization, specifically the civilization of Western Europe, from German domination; to defend and protect our declared neutral rights, especially that of freedom of the seas; and to preserve our national honor.

After the war, we attempted withdrawal, rejecting membership in the League of Nations, insisting on the settlement of war debts, and placing most of our confidence and effort in disarmament as the way to world order.

When the clear challenge of World War II came in

both Europe and Asia, we responded. After the war ended, we acknowledged a continuing responsibility to hold what had been secured and to rebuild the nations, allies and enemies alike, which had been shattered by the war. Ratification of the North Atlantic Treaty and acceptance of the Marshall Plan and of membership in the United Nations demonstrated our acceptance of new and continuing responsibility to the rest of the world.

Korea was the first real military test of our new commitment. Our response was controlled and limited. The earlier loss of China by Chiang Kai-shek to the Communists was accepted as of such magnitude as to be beyond our responsibility or prudentially measured power to recover—at least immediately.

With John Foster Dulles as Secretary of State, our moral—or at least what was declared to be moral —obligations and our legal obligations to establish justice, to redress grievances, to contain communism, to establish democracies, to maintain order—all obligations to which we were committed in measure, within the legal and moral limitations of the United Nations— were, in a broader context, taken up as special burdens of the United States. We entered unbalanced treaty arrangements, in which we were the nation of greatest strength and responsibility. We also agreed to underwrite treaties entered into by other nations such as CENTO (Central Treaty Organization).

But we did not stop at the limits of these sweeping treaty obligations, covering, if we include NATO and our bilateral defense treaties in the Far East, nearly all of Europe, most of Asia, and all of Latin America. The Eisenhower Doctrine, first applied in Lebanon where neither direct nor indirect Communist influence was present, committed us, or at least opened the way, to involvement in any disagreement, internal or external, of nearly every country in the world by the invitation of the government of that country if we accepted its invitation.

Thus we went into Lebanon in 1958, at the request of that country's government, to help settle a purely domestic political dispute.

The principle of intervention by request was incorporated in the plans for the invasion of Cuba, in that once an invasion beachhead had been established, it was planned that a self-declared Cuban government would invite the United States to help it establish and maintain order.

In somewhat the same way, in 1965, we went into the Dominican Republic, according to official United States government reports, because we were asked to by the government of the Dominican Republic to save the lives of nonresidents. We were asked to stay—or were moved to stay—and expand our military strength to prevent what was described as an imminent Communist takeover.

Today our potential foreign obligations are almost unlimited. We have moved from a position of isolation and rejection of world responsibility to a position of isolated, almost singular responsibility for the whole world.

We must, therefore, attempt to assay our real power as compared with our assumed responsibilities. We must reassess our obligations, formal and informal, legal and extra-legal. We must establish, if we can, standards for selection of responses, both as to place and degree. We must set priorities and continue to seek, with other nations, a broader and more realistic distribution of responsibility for this world.

2

Power
Through People

We are quick to assert that ours is a government of laws and not of men. This statement is generally true when it refers to the domestic affairs of the United States. It is not so clearly true when applied to foreign affairs.

The laws and rules that govern in the field of foreign affairs are stated formally in treaties and in international agreements and, less directly and less formally, in laws or resolutions approved by the Congress. In today's world, many treaties, if not most, are outmoded almost before they are signed. NATO is approximately twenty years old, and already it has shown signs of old age. France has all but withdrawn from it; other members are demanding change.

Broad direction is still given to foreign policy through constitutional processes, but modern foreign policy depends principally on the men who make it at conferences, in meetings, by executive order, or by agreements. The relationships among the nations of the world today reflect more certainly the influence of men like Roosevelt, Churchill, Truman, and Stalin than the influence of treaties, old or new.

In the United States, the President is potentially the greatest influence on foreign policy. In theory, Secretaries of State have no power excepting that which is given to them by the President. Yet by the nature of their office, because of their closeness to the President, because of their freedom to specialize in foreign policy —while a President must look to many other things— and possibly because of their greater knowledge and competence in foreign matters, modern Secretaries of State can have great influence on the policy decisions of the government.

Since 1948, in the post-World War II period, the United States has had four Presidents, Truman, Eisenhower, Kennedy, and Johnson, and three long-term Secretaries of State, Dean Acheson, John Foster Dulles, and Dean Rusk.

Dean Acheson was forty-seven years old when appointed Assistant Secretary of State in 1941. He had previously served in government only one year, in 1933, as an Undersecretary of Treasury, being replaced by Henry Morgenthau after disagreeing with President Roosevelt on the devaluation of gold.

On January 7, 1949, he was appointed Secretary of State to succeed George C. Marshall and confirmed by the Senate on January 18, 1949. Acheson was the most controversial of these three Secretaries.

Secretary Acheson and the President he served, Harry Truman, seem to have been more closely identified than the other two Secretaries and their principals. Acheson and Truman were held jointly responsible for both the good and the bad. Their popularity in the country seemed to rise and fall simultaneously. Each supported the other's views with firm commitment and strong and certain language.

Acheson seldom, if ever, made the case for policy on an ideological or idealistic basis. His approach was generally pragmatic although he was not indifferent to ethical and moral considerations. He was not a great treaty maker and he did not hesitate to circumvent or ignore collective security apparatus when necessity dictated quick or independent action, as for example, when aid to Greece and Turkey was implemented through the Truman Doctrine.

Although, as Secretary, he is reported to have had confidence in Congress initially, his attitude soon changed. Throughout most of his term as Secretary of State, he was in open conflict with the Congress, especially with the more conservative and isolationist members. He and President Truman believed in separation of powers and in fixing responsibility. They rejected the suggestion that a congressional resolution in support of the Korean War be sought.

Dean Acheson set forth most of his general views on foreign policy and on his approach to it in a speech at Amherst College on December 9, 1964. In that speech he stated:

> The end sought by our foreign policy, the purpose for which we carry on relations with foreign states is . . . to preserve and foster an environment in which free societies may exist and flourish. Our policies and actions must be tested by whether they contribute to or detract from achievement of this end. . . .

Concerned that the major pitfall of the moralist in government can be preoccupation with how a country does things rather than with what it does, he went on:

> We can never reach the point where all ends must be justified by their means before implementing policy, but we must be certain that our ends are really what we want.

Yet he was concerned about means and methods. In the Amherst speech he said:

> I take it as clear, that, where an important purpose of diplomacy is to further enduring good relations between states, the methods—the modes of conduct—by which relations between states are carried on must be designed to inspire trust and confidence. To achieve this result, the conduct of diplomacy should conform to the same moral and ethical principles which inspire trust and confidence when followed by and between individuals.

Under Acheson, the State Department was moved toward becoming a more effective operating arm of the executive branch of the government. It was during his term that a point was reached after which it has been nonsensical to say that any President is his own Secretary of State.

As Assistant Secretary and later as Undersecretary of State, Acheson was credited with helping push through the Lend-Lease bill and with making important contributions to plans for the United Nations in 1945. He worked successfully for congressional approval of the Bretton Woods Monetary Agreement and was chairman of the commission which produced the Acheson-Lilienthal report, the basis of the Baruch plan for the international control of atomic energy.

Dean Acheson deserves a large measure of credit for the formation of the International Bank for Reconstruction and Development, the United Nations Relief and Rehabilitation Administration, the United Nations Food and Agriculture Organization, and the Marshall Plan.

In 1945, shortly after becoming Undersecretary of State, Acheson spoke to the National Council of Soviet-American Friendship, saying that he saw no place on the globe where United States and Soviet interests would clash. As the cold war developed, he changed his stand. In 1947, he went before the Congress to define the Truman Doctrine and to propose United States aid to Greece and Turkey, anti-Communist programs of which he was a principal architect.

The basic Truman-Acheson policy was directed toward order in Europe. Its principal and immediate objectives were the containment of Russia and the rebuilding and incorporation of Germany into the structure of Western Europe.

The Korean War was not so much an involvement based upon the general policy of containment as it was a kind of wrapping up of World War II in the

Asian theater. The Acheson policy for Asia and for
Africa and for the Middle East was one of limited
commitment.

His conception of national defense was one of a defined perimeter, described more simply by President
Truman, when he said that any time a pig stuck his
snout under the tent, the thing to do was to hit him
on the snout. The Acheson conception of foreign policy was classical, therefore restrained and limited. He
would have been a good delegate at the Congress of
Vienna.

John Foster Dulles was a very different kind of
Secretary of State. He committed himself to foreign
service early in life and looked upon that service as a
kind of vocation. He attended the second Hague Peace
Conference in 1907 when he was only nineteen years
old. From 1911 to 1949, he was a member of the firm
of Sullivan and Cromwell, practicing principally in international law.

In 1919, he attended the Versailles Peace Conference
as an appointee of President Wilson. In 1927, he was
legal adviser to those who were planning Polish financial stabilization. In 1933, he was an American adviser at the Berlin Debt Conference; in 1945, a delegate to the San Francisco Conference on World Organization. In 1946, 1947, 1948, and 1950, he was a
member of the United States delegation to the United
Nations General Assembly. In 1951, he negotiated the
Japanese peace treaty as a special representative of
President Truman. In 1950 and 1951, he negotiated the
ANZUS treaty and the Japanese security treaty.

John Foster Dulles succeeded Dean Acheson as
Secretary of State in 1953. His approach to foreign policy was essentially moralistic and ideological.
For Dulles, neutralism *was* immoral. World conflict
was basically ideological. "The Communists," he said,

"believe they represent the wave of the future. They are fanatic in promoting this idea. We must have people on our side who believe that our way of life is the way of the future." To him, communism was a monolith and international communism "a single party."*

Whereas Acheson was the advocate, carrying his case to the country and to the Congress in open, hard conflict, Dulles was not. He laid down broad moral objectives like "peace" and "liberation." He made threats of "massive retaliation."

Dulles is quoted as saying:

> Our foreign policy can best be expressed by extending to the whole world the words of the Preamble to the Constitution of the United States— "to form a more perfect Union, establish justice, insure domestic tranquility, provide for the common defense, promote the general welfare, and secure the blessings of liberty to ourselves and our posterity. . . ."
>
> What does this mean in our international relations? "To form a more perfect Union" means to assist in making the United Nations an effective organization for peace. "Establish justice" means to strengthen international law so as to bring peace with justice. "Insure domestic tranquility" means to assist other peoples to achieve their just aspirations through peaceful change, rather than violence. "Provide for the common defense" means to join with other nations so as to protect their and our freedom from any force, particularly international communism, which seeks to destroy them. "Promote the general welfare" means to stimulate the development of the less-developed nations. "Secure the blessings of lib-

---

* Andrew H. Berding, *Dulles on Diplomacy* (Princeton, Van Nostrand, 1965), p. 63.

erty" embraces all these objectives, and it also
means we should make known to other peoples
that the American Revolution was the true revolution for human freedom.*

"We look on the world as a whole," Dulles said. "We
cannot be weak anywhere without creating danger
everywhere."†

In contrast to the limited and defined objectives of
Acheson, Dulles' view was unlimited and open-ended.
Dulles was a great treaty maker. He took credit for
strengthening NATO, for setting up SEATO, for ef-
fecting our adherence to the Military Committee of
the Baghdad Pact, and for our mutual defense treaties
with Korea, Nationalist China, and Japan. Only Latin
America and Africa were left free of special treaty
commitments, although there were rumors of an African treaty to contain Nasser and a strong assumption
that Dulles thought the Monroe Doctrine adequate
for Latin America.

In addition to signing or endorsing treaties, Dulles
was a great proponent of congressional resolutions,
which served his purposes in two ways: first, by giving
a kind of legalistic justification for action in certain
cases; second, by preventing criticism or greatly reducing its strength.

Whereas Truman and Acheson went into Korea
without special congressional action, Dulles in trouble was quick to come to the Congress. First, he presented the Far East (Formosa) Resolution in 1955,
greatly overemphasizing its legal and other effects
when he explained it:

> With Formosa threatened with attack from the
> Chinese mainland we got the Far East resolution
> passed by Congress. This put the Peiping govern-

* Berding, p. 13.
† *Ibid.*, p. 62.

ment unmistakably on notice that if it attacked Formosa the United States would instantly be in the war.*

He came to the Congress again in 1957 following the Suez crisis, asking Congress to pass the Joint Resolution on the Middle East, which stated the United States determination to assist any country in the area that asked for help if it were threatened by Communist-inspired aggression.

There were few positive achievements in foreign policy under Dulles. Treaty commitments were made. The use of congressional resolutions in support or in anticipation of foreign policy decisions was emphasized.

As Secretary, Dulles spoke of liberation, but he did not suggest support of the Hungarians in their revolt against Russia. He used the term "agonizing reappraisal" and told the Europeans that they must agree to a European Defense Community, or develop an EDC; that the alternative was nothing. Yet the NATO alliance during his term as Secretary drifted along for eight years with no significant structural change.

During the early years of the Eisenhower Administration, the United States continued indirect support of the French in Southeast Asia, but when the critical question of open military assistance, or intervention, was raised, the Administration declined.

The only open acts of intervention in the eight years of the Eisenhower Administration were the very limited defense of Quemoy and the landing of troops in Lebanon. The invasion of Cuba was also planned but not carried out, and retaliatory action against the British, French, and Israelis at the time of the Suez crisis was only threatened.

Under Dulles, the Central Intelligence Agency, directed by his brother, Allen, became a major force in

* *Ibid.*, p. 129.

formulating and executing foreign policy. Independent of the Congress, not limited by our treaty obligations, it enmeshed itself in politics, taking credit for the overthrow of Arbenz in Guatemala and Mossadegh in Iran. It was active in Laos and Vietnam, and it helped to plan and carry out the invasion of Cuba in 1960–1961.

It is too early to pass judgment on the record of Dean Rusk as Secretary of State. As Secretary of State since 1961, he has not yet made a distinct mark either as an administrator or as a policy maker.

Dean Rusk's involvement in foreign affairs was somewhat less direct and less directed than John Foster Dulles'. Rusk was an assistant professor of government at Mills College before going into the Army in 1940. In 1943, he went overseas and served in the China-Burma-India theater, eventually becoming deputy chief of staff to General Stilwell. Returning to civilian life in 1946, he served in 1946 and 1947 as Special Assistant to the Secretary of War. In 1947 and 1948 he was director of the Office of Special Political Affairs in the Department of State. He remained in that department, advancing to director of the Office of United Nations Affairs in 1948, to Assistant Secretary for United Nations Affairs in 1949, to Deputy Under-Secretary of State in 1949 and 1950, and to Assistant Secretary for Far Eastern Affairs from 1950 to 1952. In 1952, he left the State Department to become president of the Rockefeller Foundation, a position which he held until he was appointed Secretary of State in 1961 by President John F. Kennedy.

Rusk has not stated his philosophical views on foreign policy, its objectives and methods, as did both Acheson and Dulles. He seems to be guided narrowly by precedent and experience and, therefore, to be unwilling to try new ideas and ventures. He seems to pattern himself after Secretary Marshall; self-controlled, holding himself aloof from subordinates, seeking to get along with the Congress and the Pentagon.

Whereas Dulles could be unpopular while President Eisenhower remained untouched, Rusk's public acceptance—one could scarcely label it either popularity or unpopularity—is unrelated to that of the President. Under President Kennedy he was little noticed. Under Johnson, especially in relation to Vietnam, he seems to have lost no status while the President has suffered.

Few policies bear his mark. In a speech in May 1951, Rusk heralded a major shift in United States Far Eastern policy, our unyielding support for the government of Chiang Kai-shek, by that time installed on Taiwan. The Peking government, he said, "is not the government of China," and the Nationalist government "more authentically represents the views of the great body of the people of China. . . ."

With reference to Europe, Rusk has not developed or supported any new policies, with the exception of the now discarded multilateral forces proposal. Before Senator Henry Jackson's subcommittee of the Senate Committee on Government Operations, Rusk spoke of "trying to keep not just abreast of events but ahead of events," and of how diplomacy has undergone a "revolutionary transformation" when "any action taken on one important matter in one place sends a chain reaction of effect in every other important problem with which we are dealing." The record fails to reflect successful response in this period of revolutionary transition.

The Rusk position on treaties and resolutions and on relationships with Congress is not wholly clear. He cites existing treaties in support of his positions. The major treaties adopted during his incumbency, the Test Ban Treaty and the Antarctic Treaty, have been outside of or beyond the ordinary diplomatic measurement. The same is true of treaties like the recently approved Treaty on Outer Space, largely a product of the

United Nations, and the proposed treaty on nonproliferation of nuclear weapons. The use of the Tonkin Gulf Resolution in support of the extension of the Vietnam War and the more recently proposed Latin American Resolution is closer to the practices of Dulles than to those of Acheson.

Rusk appears to have a conception of the role of Secretary quite different from that of his predecessors. According to a former colleague:

> Rather than doing battle in the name of the State Department, or even representing it, Rusk seemed to see himself as standing somewhat apart, more as a personal adviser to the President than as representing any particular point of view, even the political. He seemed to view the Secretary not as the maker and advocate of policy, but, at the President's side, as a judge.*

Complaints of lack of coordination and lack of control within the State Department continue. The relationship of the Department of State with the Congress, or at least with the Foreign Relations Committee of the Senate, grows worse. The CIA has not been well directed. The growing influence of the Department of Defense, not only in Vietnam but on policy making as well, particularly with reference to arms distribution around the world, becomes clearer.

Rusk's administration and practical record are also subject to challenge. The Cuban invasion occurred while he was Secretary. Relationships with France and NATO could not have been handled more ineptly, and Vietnam continues as a test of a Secretary who has yet to make his mark.

* Roger Hilsman, *To Move a Nation* (Garden City, N.Y., Doubleday, 1967), p. 59.

3

Power Through Gunpowder

The foreign policy of the United States is a product of many forces: defense of the national interest, the national security, idealism, the desire for trade. Other considerations, however, influence policy in a very real although less direct manner. One element is what might be called the factor of inertia, the tendency of programs to continue beyond the situation that brought them into being. Programs decided upon in years past to support specific objectives of the national interest can assume a kind of life of their own; they tend to become vested interests which may be self-perpetuating.

Over the years, the Military Assistance Program appears to have assumed such a character. Inaugurated to respond to the military challenge of the cold war in Europe, there is evidence that its survival today tends to put a military mark on American foreign policy and to create situations and conditions that lead the United States to react in military terms when a political response is preferable. In my judgment, it is one of the most important aspects of our foreign policy. Yet, it has received relatively little attention.

The United States is today the principal source of conventional weapons throughout the world. The United States government, largely through its military assistance and arms sales program, is the world's leading supplier of arms. The United States government itself has today assumed the role filled by the widely scorned munitions makers during the interwar period.

The United States was a supplier of limited assistance to friendly nations for many years before World War II, notably through our loans to the Allies during the First World War. Just prior to World War

II, the Lend-Lease Program, adopted in March of
1941, permitted the President "to authorize the manu-
facture of defense articles . . . for any foreign government whose defense he deemed vital to the defense
of the United States" and to "sell, transfer title to, exchange, lease, lend, or otherwise dispose of to any such
government any defense article." The United States
thus took its first step toward becoming the great
arsenal of democracy, enlarging its own defense
capacity while supplying British needs.

With the entry of the United States into the Second
World War, Lend-Lease deliveries were speeded up,
and by the end of the war, their dollar value exceeded
$48.5 billion. Although assistance was given to forty-
two countries, the principal beneficiaries were the
British Empire ($32 billion), the Soviet Union ($11
billion), and France (approximately $3 billion).

With the development of a Soviet military threat to
Europe following World War II, the United States
entered into the North Atlantic Treaty. It was evident,
however, that a war-torn and economically prostrate
Europe could not maintain sufficient defense capability
to deter the Soviet threat. The United States, therefore,
under the Mutual Defense Assistance Act of October 6,
1949, began to provide grant military aid of three
types: (1) machinery and materials to permit Europe
to increase its own production of defense items; (2)
direct transfer of U.S. military equipment; and (3) assistance in the production and use of military equipment and training of personnel.

Under the successive foreign aid acts, these three
forms of military assistance have remained at the
center of our aid programs. Between 1950 and 1966,
the United States gave other nations over $35 billion
worth of military materials and support under our
foreign aid program. Recently the trend has been to
arms *sales* rather than to continue grants and transfers.

Prior to 1955, the United States and Britain had a virtual monopoly in supplying modern weapons to those areas that were not directly involved in the cold war conflict. The Soviet Union was concentrating on arming her allies in Eastern Europe, China, and North Korea. The European powers had not yet sufficiently recovered from the devastation of the Second World War to have developed their own weapons production.

France, long a supplier of arms to the Middle East, is now reported to be exporting nearly 40 percent of her total aerospace production. Great Britain is actively engaged in arms sales competition with the United States, particularly in Latin America.

In 1965, Britain and France are reported to have sold about $700 million worth of arms throughout the world; the Soviet Union provided approximately $400 million worth of equipment to countries in the Middle East, Africa, Asia, and the Caribbean.*

The efforts of France, Britain, and even of the Soviet Union remain small compared with those of the United States.

Our commercial sales total, that is, sales abroad of military equipment by United States industry and commercial suppliers, is not known precisely. The State Department, which has the responsibility for licensing "the export and import of arms, ammunition, and implements of war" under the Mutual Security Act of 1954, does not maintain statistical compilations of these transactions, making weapons one of the few products of American industry on which official export quantity data are not readily obtainable. According to the 1967 Senate Foreign Relations Committee Staff Study, *Arms Sales and Foreign Policy*, the U.S. Defense Department's sales abroad totaled $1.97 billion in Fiscal Year 1965 and around $1.93 billion in Fiscal

* Geoffrey Kemp, "Arms Sales and Arms Control in Developing Countries," *The World Today* (London), September 1966.

Year 1966. According to the Defense Department, the United States program of grants plus sales has been running around $3 billion per year since 1961.

Over eighty countries have received either grant aid (gift), sales, or training assistance through the Military Assistance Program.

We provide arms, equipment, and training to countries allied or associated with us through the North Atlantic Treaty and through a network of pacts and treaties, such as SEATO (Southeast Asia Treaty Organization), CENTO (Central Treaty Organization), ANZUS (Australia, New Zealand, United States Security Pact).

In addition to treaty assistance, we have provided military aid to a wide range of countries in such categories as "forward defense areas," that is, countries on or adjacent to the borders of the Communist world, including the Republic of China (Taiwan), Iran, the Philippines, South Korea, Greece, and Turkey (the last two countries are also allied to us through NATO); to countries that have given us military base rights, such as Ethiopia, Libya, Spain, and our NATO ally Portugal; to the "Alliance for Progress security countries"— virtually every country in Latin America; and to additional countries in Asia, Africa, and the Middle East which have, or which are judged to have, what is described by the Defense Department as a "free world orientation."

The stage for conflict in the Middle East was set long ago. Between 1950 and 1965, the United States supplied relatively small amounts of grant military assistance to the Middle East: to Iraq, $46.5 million; to Jordan, $33 million; to Saudi Arabia, $31 million. But during 1965 we began to move away from our traditional policy of attempting to avoid becoming a major supplier of arms to the Middle East and, at least until the outbreak of war in June 1967, we were deeply involved in bolstering both Israel and the Arab states against each other as well as in building up the Saudi Arabians and the Iranians against Nasser.

A higher proportion of resources is spent for military purposes in the Middle East than anywhere else in the developing world. Aircraft strengths in particular increased rapidly during 1965–1966. The Israelis have acquired their aircraft largely from the French, but in 1966 they were promised U.S. Skyhawk bombers, the first offensive weapon the United States introduced into the area.

The stated reason for the promise of U.S. bombers to Israel was to build up their deterrent against the Egyptians, whose air force has been supplied by the Soviet Union, and includes MIG-21's, one of the most advanced Soviet jet fighters. Iraq and Syria have also been supplied by the Soviet Union in smaller amounts. The Jordanians had a small number of British aircraft, but in 1966 were promised about thirty-six U.S. Starfighter jets. It is not clear as to how Jordan, an economically nonviable country with an annual per capita Gross National Product of $233, dependent on U.S. military grants and economic aid to meet her budget, will pay for these planes, which cost some two million dollars apiece.

The British, often in competition with the United States in the arms sales business, are cooperating with us to provide Saudi Arabia with a $400 million air defense system, of which the U.S. component will be the HAWK missile. We had previously provided Israel with the HAWK missile.

Most serious of all, perhaps, was the U.S. decision in late 1966 to sell to Iran a squadron of F-4 Phantoms, our most sophisticated operational supersonic aircraft, a decision which may precipitate a new round in the Middle East arms race.

An important consideration in the decision to sell arms to Iran was the desire to dissuade the Shah from seeking Soviet arms, an example of "pre-emptive sell-ing" which appears to be an increasingly important aspect of the U.S. arms sales program.* A few months later, however, it became known that the Shah had concluded a military assistance agreement with the Soviet Union and would be receiving Soviet arms.

The case of Iran also demonstrates the changing motives of the arms supply program. Aid to Iran has traditionally been justified on the basis of its strategic and exposed position on the frontier of the Soviet Union. Recently, however, the Defense Department has said that the main reason for arms sales to Iran is to bolster the Shah against the threat of "Arab nation-alism."

There are other arms races of potential danger in the area. Morocco has been displaying its first American-built jets, and maintains that it requires even more for defense against Algeria, which has been receiving Soviet arms.

In mid-1967, following the brief war in which American weapons were used by both sides, the Ad-ministration began a review of our arms supply policy for the Middle East.

Ethiopia has received more U.S. military aid than any other African nation, $107.6 million between 1950 and 1966, which is as much as the other African nations put together received. We have an important communications base in Ethiopia which has served as a justification for the provision of large amounts of aid. An arms race in the Horn of Africa, the area bordering the Red Sea and the Gulf of Aden, is a potential dan-ger. The Soviet Union has long sought to gain a toe-hold in the Red Sea region, and has been supplying arms to Somalia, which has a long-standing dispute with Ethiopia over the Ogaden district of Ethiopia and over territory in Kenya.

* The New York *Times*, September 19, 1966.

Tensions among the Latin American states are not high at present. But our Military Assistance Program, through grant aid, and increasingly through sales, appears to be expanding, in spite of attempts by Congress to put some limits on it.

The Congress, particularly the Senate, has been increasingly critical of the level of the military assistance and sales programs to Latin America.

A new round in the arms race, moving from subsonic jets in the direction of the more sophisticated and more expensive supersonic jets, was apparently precipitated by the U.S. decision in 1965 to provide fifty U.S. Skyhawks to Argentina. One explanation was that we hoped to appease the Argentine military so that they would be less inclined to overthrow the civilian government. A military coup did take place, however, on June 28, 1966, and on the same day the United States reduced the promised number of planes to twenty-five, claiming that they were needed for Vietnam. (The sale of twenty-five planes was allowed to go through.)

The Chilean military, moved by what Argentina had been promised, pressed their government to acquire planes of comparable sophistication and, when refused by the United States, the Chileans made a deal with the British for planes. This, in turn, inspired reaction by Venezuela, which began negotiations for some U.S.-model jets from West Germany; Peru began negotiating with the United States, France, and Britain for planes; and Brazil also was reported to be in the market.

The Argentine case illustrates what appears to be a major consideration in the Military Assistance Program in Latin America, the presumption that the success of United States policy depends on recognition and support of a special role for the military in many Latin American countries.

State Department officials are always quick to point

out that in percentage terms Latin American defense budgets are small, "among the lowest in the world," as former Assistant Secretary of State Lincoln Gordon has stated. And Secretary of Defense McNamara, before the Senate Foreign Relations Committee in 1966, pointed out that the number of tanks in Latin America was only 60 percent of the number in Bulgaria. But what is important is not the percentage, but the fact that money that should be spent for social and economic development is being sacrificed to pay for even relatively small quantities of arms.

Moreover, the cost of military aid in Latin America is not only monetary. As one writer has put it:

> The political cost is apparent in the case of Brazil. The social result of aiding the generals is another often overlooked factor. . . . But even the economic cost is appalling. . . . The U.S. may only provide $80 million or so annually in actual arms (forgetting the dozens of missions, joint maneuvers, etc., which the Pentagon subsidizes). But today it costs twice as much annually ($2 billion) to keep the region's "gorillas" happy as it receives in *Alianza* aid.*

The case of India and Pakistan has frequently been cited as the outstanding example of the damage the Military Assistance Program can do. It "caused the war" between those two countries, J. Kenneth Galbraith told the Senate Foreign Relations Committee in 1966. Mr. Galbraith, our former Ambassador to India, is one of the men most familiar with that situation.

Pakistan, which has recently been receiving military assistance and arms from Communist China, is formally allied to us through SEATO and is reported to have received from $1.5 to $2 billion in U.S. military

---

* Donald D. Ranstead, "Arms Race in Latin America," *Commonweal*, December 16, 1966.

assistance over the decade prior to the outbreak of war in 1965, allegedly for defense against communism. India refused U.S. military aid until her borders were attacked by China, but she had been receiving arms from the United Kingdom. In the end United States arms were used by both sides against each other.

U.S. arms deliveries to India and Pakistan were suspended at the time of the fighting. On the strength of the adherence of the two countries to the Tashkent Agreement, deliveries have been resumed on what the State Department calls "a case-by-case basis." Despite criticism of arms sales and deliveries by the Congress and others, there is little evidence of a change of policy.

U.S. government funds are also used to promote arms sales; in Fiscal Year 1965, $500,000 of military assistance funds was programmed for sales *promotion*. The Director of the Military Assistance Program, General Robert Wood, explained to the House Appropriations Committee in 1964 that the training program is the foot in the door for the arms salesman. "We bring officers over here from other countries," General Wood explained, "with a view to looking at equipment which they might buy. . . . Then we have a program to train certain countries in some of our equipment in the expectation they will buy the equipment. This is really sales promotion."

The Pentagon has been pressing the U.S. defense industry to take an even greater interest in the overseas market. Henry Kuss, Deputy Assistant Secretary for International Logistics Negotiations, the Pentagon's chief arms salesman, in a speech to the American Ordnance Association in October 1966, stated:

> The tendency of American companies to refrain from entering into the international arms market is a serious one and affects our entire international

posture in a military, economic, and political way.

From the military point of view we stand to lose all of the major relationships paid for with grant money unless we can establish professional military relationships through the sales media. . . .

He then went on to cite the problem of the balance of payments. Increasing trade is, of course, most important as far as our balance of payments is concerned. But, if the U.S. weapons industry has grown to such proportions in relation to the nonmilitary sectors of American industry that only by further expansion of arms sales can we meet our balance of payments problems, then I would suggest that there is serious cause for concern.

Statistics can be misleading. For example, Secretary McNamara maintained that the Defense Department's request for less than one billion dollars for the Military Assistance Program for Fiscal Year 1967 was in line with the recommendations of the Clay Committee that the program should be reduced. But the money appropriated by Congress is only for the grant-aid (that is, weapons given without expectation of reimbursement) and credit-assistance portions of the program. Grant-aid programs for Europe are being replaced by sales programs, and sales are playing an increasingly large role in the programs for the developing countries. Because of the decrease in grant aid to European countries, it has been possible to increase programs in other areas, while still appearing to reduce the total budget request. Thus, in 1956, Ethiopia was the only country in Africa receiving military grant aid, in the amount of $4 million. By 1961 the number of African countries in which there were at least small programs totaled seven; in 1962 it had increased to fifteen countries—the Ethiopian program having more than doubled to $10.9 million and the total for the continent having increased fourfold, from the $4 million figure in 1956 to $17.8 million in 1962. In 1963 the total for grant-aid military assistance to Africa rose to $26 million, in 1964 to nearly $28 million. In 1965 it dropped to $17.4 million, but for 1967 the Administration requested a total of $31.8 million, the highest figure ever. These figures are not large in absolute terms, but when one considers the level of development of the countries involved—Mali, with a per capita Gross National Product of $65, Guinea with $70, Liberia with $175, and Sudan with $102—it can be seen that in such areas even a small number of arms can be highly significant.

Latin America shows a similar increase in the grant-aid program. Prior to 1956, it operated in only ten countries, and in the years between 1950 and 1955, a total of $77.3 million worth of assistance was provided. In addition, some countries were able to purchase arms. In the single year of 1956, a total of $23.3 million worth of military assistance was given to twelve countries. In 1961, twenty countries received a total of $44 million in grant aid. These included Venezuela, which had always paid for what it received but which now was receiving a small amount of gift military aid. Also in 1961, Cuba was credited with receiving $100,000 worth, a Defense Department payment for material delivered several years previously.

By 1965, we were operating a $55.8 million grant-aid program in eighteen Latin American countries and Jamaica. (The suspension of the Cuba and Haiti programs was responsible for the reduction in the number of countries.) In 1966, the Administration requested almost $80 million for Latin America. The existing law imposed a ceiling of $55 million on the grant of defense articles to Latin America. But, as the Senate Foreign Relations Committee found in examining the Administration's request, this was only part of the story. According to the 1966 committee report on the military aid bill:

The importance of applying the limitation to all types of assistance except training is shown in the proposed fiscal 1967 program for Latin America. A total of $74.9 million in grant aid has been programmed, of which only $50.4 million, the amount scheduled for grants of defense articles, would count against the $55 million ceiling in existing law.

The balance is made of $12.3 million for training, and $12.2 million in grants of other defense services. In addition, sales of $71.5 million are contemplated. Thus, the total military assistance and sales program in 1967 would amount to $146.4 million. Under existing law, $96 million of this amount would be exempt from the ceiling. Under the committee bill, only the training expenses of $12.3 million will be exempt, and this will force a considerable reduction in the program.

In the budget presentations to Congress, the entire program of military assistance to Vietnam for Fiscal Year 1967 was removed from the military assistance budget and incorporated into the budget of the Defense Department because, as Administration officials testified, the sums for Vietnam were now so large that they were "distorting" the Military Assistance Program. For Fiscal Year 1968, expenditures for Laos and Thailand and for such other categories as NATO infrastructure and support for international organizations were also moved from the military assistance budget to the regular Defense Department budget on similar grounds. These budgeting changes weaken political control of these programs, which involve essential considerations of foreign policy, and make them subject almost entirely to Defense Department control.

Alastair Buchan, Director of the Institute of Strategic Studies in Britain, wrote in *The New Republic* on November 6, 1965:

> The private trade in arms, the grubby activities of the men in Alexandria and Monaco, Milan and Hamburg, who can supply a plane load of rifles or a couple of old aircraft to a rebel leader, are not a serious threat to international peace. It is the sober policy of sober governments which is the root of the trouble.

The formal Military Assistance Program is at present carried out under the authority of the Foreign Assistance Act of 1961, under the direction and supervision of the Secretary of State. Theoretically, the Secretary of Defense has responsibility for the operating level and for technical aspects of the program. The Defense Department works closely with the United States defense industry to promote the sale abroad of U.S. military equipment and services, both on a direct commercial basis and through the Defense Department's procurement system.

Although the Secretary of State has official responsibility for the military assistance and arms sales program, the tendency of this program to move ahead at its own momentum has caused serious questions to be raised as to whether this political control is effective. The 1967 study by the Senate Foreign Relations Committee staff suggested that control was more theoretical than real:

> How and by whom the major decisions on arms sales are made is something of a mystery. There is reported to be a State-Defense Coordinating Committee for arms sales policy consisting of members of Treasury, the State Department, the Defense Department, and presumably the Arms Control Agency and AID. Whether the full Com-

mittee actually meets is uncertain. One thing is
clear, however, from testimony the Foreign Relations Committee has already heard: the Arms
Control and Disarmament Agency, despite its
charter, does not sit at the high table when decisions on the sale of arms are made. Another open
question is whether the Agency for International
Development or the Bureau of the Budget actually
participate in the progress of making a decision
to sell . . . or have only the option of attempting
to overturn a promise of arms sales already made
to another country.

A program of this magnitude is bound to have im-
plications for our foreign policy. United States military
aid is usually, if not invariably, accompanied by the
stationing of U.S. military personnel in the country receiving the arms to supervise, advise, assist, and draw
up plans, in accordance with Defense Department pro-
cedures, for the utilization by the country of additional
U.S. equipment. These U.S. military advisers act as
on-the-spot salesmen, attempting to make certain that
the country concerned obtains its military equipment
from the United States and not from a competitor,
political or commercial. These military advisers sometimes assume more direct roles.

The object of the training aspect of the program is
to get other countries to use our methods and equipment and to establish good relations with those who
will be tomorrow's procurement offices or tomorrow's
military leaders.

The future leaders of many countries of the world
are first exposed to the United States within a military
frame of reference. Between 1951 and 1966, the number of grants for foreigners to study in the United
States in all academic disciplines was 125,880.* For

* Includes some for whom the U.S. government provided only
partial support.

about the same period, the number of individuals who completed formal training at United States expense under the Military Assistance Program was 259,980. Defense Department officials have frequently cited the importance of military assistance training as a vehicle for exposing foreigners to the American way of life. Almost twice as many foreigners are trained in the military program as in all academic disciplines put together.

Most of the arms supplied by the Defense Department under the grant-aid and sales portions of the Military Assistance Program have gone to the industrialized countries of Western Europe and Asia. But an alarming increase has taken place, particularly within the past few years, in the number and quality of arms we supply to the developing countries, the countries which are least able to afford them or which are able to acquire them only by diverting precious resources from nonmilitary development programs.

The question of whether the U.S. government ought to be promoting the sale of U.S. arms abroad, particularly to the developing countries, is one of considerable complexity. It can be answered only by weighing the positive and negative aspects of the program.

One of the chief positive features, in the eyes of the defenders of the program, is its use as an important element of United States foreign policy. Secretary of Defense Robert McNamara, in testimony before the Senate Committee on Foreign Relations in April 1966, described its role:

> For more than 17 years, the United States has built its foreign policy on a program of economic and military assistance to friendly nations. This policy has been a success. It has held Soviet and Red Chinese expansionism in check, and it has

helped many of our allies and other friendly nations toward self-sustaining growth. . . .

The governing principle of our Military Assistance Program has been and is that the vital interests of this country in the defense of the free world are dependent upon the strength of the entire free world and not merely upon the strength of the United States.

The United States is the focus of power in the free world struggle for national independence and economic progress; but the United States cannot be everywhere at once, doing everything the best. The balance of forces and the options necessary in today's challenging world can be achieved only with staunch friends, well armed and ready to do their parts of the job.

The Military Assistance Program is designed to foster that balance of forces and those options. It helps support military forces that complement our own Armed Forces.

Military assistance provides essential arms, training, and related support to some 5 million men in allied and other friendly forces, who help us hold the line against aggression in all its forms and guises. These men are critical to our forward strategy.

That the Vietnam War does not sustain this argument is perhaps the most obvious challenge to the validity of Secretary McNamara's case. The "5 million men" are nowhere to be seen, while the United States has committed in Southeast Asia over half a million men, exactly the kind of situation from which the Military Assistance Program, according to Secretary McNamara, is supposed to save us. As far as the "staunch friends, well armed and ready to do their parts of the job" are concerned, one may again cite Vietnam. Few countries have received as much U.S.

assistance as has Vietnam, both during the French colonial period and since. Yet, by all evidence, despite over a decade of U.S. training and supply, the South Vietnamese army is unable and perhaps unwilling to fight, has been incompetently led, is crippled by an enormous rate of desertion, and is essentially incapable of even providing security in key areas, while the Americans bear the brunt of the fighting.

Another major argument in favor of the Military Assistance Program is carried over from the John Foster Dulles era: the "great arc theory." The series of defense pacts, such as the Baghdad Pact (CENTO) and SEATO, formed during the Dulles era was an application of the theory that one could somehow contain communism with an "arc of steel" encircling the Soviet Union and China. The ink was scarcely dry on Dulles' pacts before the Russians demonstrated their ability to leap over the "walls of steel" by their move to establish influence in Egypt and Indonesia. The *military* pacts were not able to cope with these essentially *political* challenges.

Still the theory of the arc persists, and thus Secretary McNamara informed the Senate Foreign Relations Committee in 1966:

> It would be unbearably costly to the United States in both money and human resources to maintain a credible force by itself along all of the great arc of forward positions to the west, south, and east of the U.S.S.R. and Red China.
>
> Still, the free world cannot leave large gaps in that arc. The solution to the problem has been a combination of forces—a mix of local forces in the homelands and of U.S. and other friendly forces ready for rapid deployment.

The great arc theory is involved in what is sometimes referred to as our "forward strategy," the strategy of confining the Soviet Union and China within their present boundaries by building up the military strength of countries on their borders.

The Military Assistance Program in Latin America, it is argued, differs from that in other areas in its emphasis on civic action as a justification for increased spending. Civic action refers to the use of local military forces in nonmilitary projects of benefit to the country, such as road construction, digging of wells, and so forth.

The emphasis on civic action is a product of the Defense Department theory of counterinsurgency reflected in the vast apparatus of quasi-academic social science research organizations supported by the department's research and development budget. The counterinsurgency theory accepts that insurgency is the product of such conditions as poverty and an unfavorable public image of the government, particularly of the military. Civic action is preventive action, it is said, and will discourage popular support for insurgency and improve the image of the military among the general population. As applied to Latin America, in particular, the civic action theory is based on the widely accepted presumption among the "tough-minded liberals" that in Latin America the armed forces constitute the one stable and democratic element and are a potential instrument for social change.

In his book *Generals vs. Presidents,* however, Edwin Lieuwen disagrees with this theory:

Today's officers are lower-middle class in social origin, but their institutional identification is so strong that it obliterates any meaningful identification with civilian social groups. Institutional considerations, the traditional insistence upon law and order, and the almost morbid fear of a social revolution that might destroy their organization combine in a political philosophy that is basically conservative. Today's military elite hews to no exotic foreign ideology. Rather, it merely responds to indigenous political conditions. It approves of reform but only at a pace moderate enough to avoid the threat of social disintegration and political chaos. . . . Militarism in Latin American today, in contrast to both Communism and democracy, is a political force that, on balance, brings social change and reform programs to a halt. It does not, therefore, constitute an alternative choice in the process of social revolution; it merely holds up that revolution.

As a recent study* has pointed out, the effect of civic action in the Latin American countries has not been proved and may at best be of only transitory value. Where U.S. military missions have evaluated the effects of civic action, this study shows, the reports usually state that it has improved the image of the military but cite as evidence only an increase in favorable publicity in the press.

The realization that both USIA and the United States military missions' public information officers help to get civic-action items placed in the press—and urge the host government's military elements to be "public relations conscious"—tends to diminish the significance of this as evidence of improvement of the military image.

The study further states that "there is very little evidence to support the conclusions . . . except for lack of insurgency in the areas where impact-type projects are underway. . . ." and that observers are often the first to admit that the absence of insurgency

* Willard F. Barber and C. Neale Ronning, *Internal Security and Military Power: Counterinsurgency and Civic Action in Latin America* (Ohio State University Press, 1966).

may not be related to the civic action programs.

A basic unanswered question is whether support of the military in Latin America is, in the long run, in the United States interest. In such countries as Guatemala, Nicaragua, and Honduras, civic action appears to be a means of institutional self-preservation for the military. And one must question the desirability of anything that strengthens the hand of those who conceive their role as involving the duty to overthrow constitutional government on grounds of which they alone are the judges or who demand the preservation of special prerogatives and conservative policies as their price for permitting the survival of constitutional government. In such cases, the immediate benefits of civic action projects may well be outweighed by the long-run disadvantages of sustaining the military as a supraconstitutional force, a policy which the United States rejects in theory.

In any event, it should be noted that in spite of the emphasis on civic action programs in Latin America by Administration officials the amounts of money devoted to civic action have been small. Fourteen percent of the Military Assistance Program proposed for Latin America for Fiscal Year 1967 was allocated for civic action; the remainder was for military equipment. This compares with approximately 10 percent for civic action in 1966, 13.7 percent in 1965, and 16.3 percent in 1964. Comparing the figures for 1965 and 1966, one finds that the percentage of military assistance funds for civic action decreased in eleven countries and increased in six, one country remaining at the same percentage level. With the exception of Guatemala (25%), Paraguay (39%), Peru (31%), and Brazil (11%), civic action programs in all Latin American countries were below 10 percent in 1966.

The rest of the program in Latin America, according to the law, is supposed to be for internal security purposes only, but it has not been possible for the

Congress to hold the executive branch to that policy. At the 1966 Senate Foreign Relations Committee hearing on military aid, when asked what the fifty Skyhawk bombers have to do with internal security in Argentina, Secretary McNamara admitted, "The answer is nothing—absolutely nothing." He then defended the sale by saying that, had we not sold the Argentines the planes, they would have bought them from another nation (presumably Britain) at a higher price.

Henry Kuss, the head of arms sales for the Defense Department, testifying before the House Foreign Affairs Committee in 1966, cited what he called the significant relationship of these arms sales to our foreign relations:

> Military sales are . . . small in terms of our total annual defense spending, accounting for less than 4 percent of the total. However, at the same time, receipts from military sales account for about one-half of the deployment costs of our forces, measured in balance-of-payment terms. The ability of this country to follow a forward strategy is heavily influenced by the balance-of-payments costs attributable to such a strategy. Thus, foreign military sales are of major interest to the Nation because they facilitate arrangements for our security throughout the world.

This balance of payments argument is curiously circular. Unmentioned is any consideration of the way in which further proliferation of conventional arms throughout the world, by contributing to rising tensions and by serving as the somewhat provocative mechanism by which we attempt to set up bastions on the very borders of the Soviet Union and China, makes the deployment of troops and our forward strategy necessary.

Moreover, as sales to developing countries accounted for only about 12 percent of total sales in recent years, and these are mostly on credit, the loss of the entire developing-country market by the United States would not make an appreciable dent in cash receipts.

The Senate Committee on Foreign Relations dealt with the balance of payments argument in its report on the 1966 Military Assistance and Sales bill, stating its view that "the U.S. balance of payments is not in such a perilous condition that it has to be salvaged by taking blood money from poorer countries."

If this forward strategy is to remain a necessary feature of our policy, it might be wiser to seek other means of offsetting its effect on the balance of payments than by pressing arms on either eager or reluctant allies.

There is increasing disparity, in my judgment, between the stated and real aims of our military assistance efforts and a widening gap between the program and the requirements of the world situation it was designed to meet. The principal purpose of our military aid, whether it be in the form of grants or sales, is said to be to strengthen the defenses of the free world against Communist aggression and subversion. But over the years significant changes have occurred in the program.

Military assistance today, as distinguished from Lend-Lease assistance under which we supplied arms to our World War II allies, has taken on new and far-reaching characteristics. It has greatly increased in quantity and has spread over a large geographical area as the number of independent nations in the world has grown. But the qualitative changes in the program may be of even greater significance.

First, military aid is no longer confined to containing communism or to short-term, "one-shot" arrangements or even to the supply of weapons. Rather we now undertake relatively long-term programs of continuing cooperation with the recipient state, involving a high degree of institutionalization, with exchange programs for training and with the dispatch of military missions to reside in the countries receiving the arms, to supervise their use as "advisers," and to turn out annually five-year plans for acquisition of additional U.S. equipment.

Second, the type and range of aid appear to have changed. The United States program not only provides the basic material and services required to establish and maintain armed forces, but also the direction and planning for long-term improvement, modernization, and development of the military capability of the country. Thus programs that began with training only have moved, as plans for development and modernization proceed, into the area of equipment acquisition with our encouragement. A frequent argument presented to support expenditures for weapons is that the money is really being used only to "modernize" the forces or to replace out-of-date or obsolete equipment. We know from the requirements of our own armed forces that obsolescence and modernization are open-ended and relative conditions.

Third, the goals of military assistance efforts appear to have undergone change. In spite of assurances by Administration spokesmen that the existence of well-supplied troops on the borders of the Communist world—even as far from it as Africa and Latin America—adds to the strength of the free world and relieves the pressure on the United States to keep even greater numbers of Americans under arms, few people believe that U.S.-equipped Iranians, or South Koreans, or Greeks, not to mention Bolivians or Peruvians, actually deter the Soviet Union or China. Our deterrent is nuclear, and the strength of our "staunch friends," to use Secretary McNamara's phrase, particularly those in the developing countries, does not add measurably to the strength of that deterrent.

The objectives of military assistance now seem to be to develop client states, to erect military-political bastions, to preserve (or to upset) regional balances of power, and increasingly to maintain friendly or favored regimes against internal subversion usually defined as Communist subversion.

One of the real motivations behind the military aid program is political. It is based, it seems, on the premise that every country not overtly controlled by Moscow or Peking should have at least a small military aid program, a premise consistently rejected by the Congress.

As Senate Majority Leader Mike Mansfield expressed it during the Senate debate on military assistance in July 1966, "We have a habit of trying to get our fingers into every corner of the globe. I think we do that too often, sometimes too heavily, and perhaps a little restraint in the other direction might be beneficial in the years ahead."

This total program comes very close in operation to being the military-industrial complex against which President Eisenhower warned just before he left office.

Critics have charged that the Military Assistance Program is no more than a dumping ground for supplies by the U.S. war machine and that it is a means for keeping U.S. military production and profits high. I believe this to be an overstatement, in spite of the fact that Secretary McNamara and his staff have frequently cited the beneficial effects and profits from the Military Assistance Program for U.S. industry and the man-hours of employment it generates.

But the very close cooperation between the Department of Defense and the arms industry bears watching. Through the Committee on Military Exports of the

Defense Industry Advisory Council, the Defense Department and other government agencies with responsibilities in the military-export field work closely with industry and private banks in promoting, negotiating, and supporting the export of U.S. military products. In the Defense Department's view, this committee provides a forum for the exchange of ideas between government and industry, and advises the Secretary of Defense on ways of maintaining U.S. military exports at a high level and on policies and activities of the U.S. government that would facilitate U.S. defense industry efforts for increased sales.

Apart from the Committee on Military Exports, which is headed by Mr. Kuss, there is close cooperation on the working level between Military Assistance Program personnel and the private defense industry. Such cooperation exists in many nonmilitary fields and is an effective mechanism—frequently the indispensable ingredient—for some of our most important national programs.

The arms sales program has also raised questions because of some of its financial practices. Most of the industrialized countries that have been buying arms in recent years have paid cash; but for the developing countries credit sales outweigh cash sales by about seven to one. These credit sales are made possible by the Defense Department's capacity to provide credit and guarantee payment by the United States government of private loans should the purchaser default. Thus countries which would normally not be considered acceptable credit risks on the commercial money market or by the Export-Import Bank are able to obtain credit for arms purchases; repayment is guaranteed by the full faith and credit of the government of the United States. By law, the Defense Department is required to keep as a reserve only one-quarter of the amount of the loan it guarantees. Thus, the Defense

Department's revolving credit account, which has grown to $383 million by 1967, supports well over one billion dollars in arms sales on credit.

Another credit source is the Export-Import Bank, which gives the Defense Department a kind of blank check for arms sales credit. Because the Defense Department is guaranteeing repayment, the Export-Import Bank, if it prefers not to know where the money is going, can shut its eyes.

Although the Defense Department is not required by law to charge any interest at all for credit arms purchases, most of the Pentagon-guaranteed loans made by the Export-Import Bank bear an interest rate of 5½ percent. Pentagon-guaranteed commercial loans for arms sales may bear interest rates as high as 9 percent and are usually short-term, thus adding substantially to the already burdensome external debt service requirements of the developing countries. Some of the same countries that have complained that 3 percent is too high an interest rate for economic-development loans have been willing to pay as much as 9 percent for nonproductive arms loans.

Defense Department spokesmen have repeatedly stated their determination to maintain arms sales at the $1.5 billion per year level or better. This must be challenged.

The Federal Republic of Germany purchased over three billion dollars' worth of arms from the United States from 1962 to 1966. The Germans agreed to these arms purchases to offset the cost to the United States, in balance of payments terms, of maintaining our troops in Germany, costs that have been running about $775 million a year. These so-called offset obligations have been resisted by the Germans in spite of the fact that one of the four "teams" into which the Pentagon's arms sales office is divided devotes itself almost exclusively to selling military equipment to Germany. In recent years, the Germans attempted to obtain United States agreement to their satisfying the offset obligations by purchases of materials other than arms, in which they feel they are adequately supplied, but the Defense Department has been insisting they buy more arms.

The failure of German Chancellor Ludwig Erhard to obtain concessions from the United States on this matter appears to have been a factor in the dispute that provoked the German government crisis of late 1966 and resulted in Erhard's removal.

German ability to absorb additional arms is limited and they have been shipping their "surplus" arms to other areas. In early 1967, the United States reportedly abandoned the effort to require additional German arms purchases in favor of other means by which Germany might help offset the cost of troops.

The Defense Department's guidelines for its arms salesmen give little encouragement to those who favor restraint. It seems that the arms sales business will be better than ever, and more and more dangerous. The high sales figures of 1966 were accounted for largely by purchases by our European allies, purchases which are not likely to be repeated. Thus, to maintain the high sales figures, the Pentagon's arms salesmen will be forced to look increasingly to the developing countries, thereby adding more fuel to the fire of the world's trouble spots.

The Defense Department pamphlet, *Information and Guidance on Military Assistance,* states:

> The Defense Department has embarked on an intensified military assistance sales program. . . .

> Achievement of . . . objectives calls for a very substantial increase over past sales levels. Success in this endeavor will be dependent in large measure upon effective sales promotion. The Defense Department has taken several steps to assist in

the successful conclusion of military sales. . . . Foreign customer preference for U.S. material is being generated by developing an appreciation of its technical superiority, price, availability, and the offer of follow-on support through U.S. logistics systems.

In many cases, credit arrangements may be made to facilitate military sales, on short or long term basis as needed.

At the same time, an assistant director of the U.S. Arms Control and Disarmament Agency admitted to the Senate Foreign Relations Committee that there was no formal consultation with his agency on Defense Department sales, that that agency's opinion on the advisability of the sale of jet fighters to Iran had not been requested, and that it did not have the kind of relationship with the Defense Department that permitted coordination on these matters.

Yet President Johnson proposed to the Disarmament Conference meeting in Geneva in 1966 that "countries, on a regional basis, explore ways to limit competition among themselves for costly weapons often sought for reasons of illusory prestige." On April 19, 1966, the United States delegate to the Disarmament Conference elaborated further the principles by which nations might undertake, on a regional basis, to limit conventional arms.

It seems to be a case where the right hand of the government, in this case the Defense Department, does not seem to know what the left hand, the arms control agency, is doing or trying to do, for it is busily promoting what the other agency is supposed to be controlling.

In several areas of the world, the supply of arms has seriously exacerbated tensions and threatened world peace. Some of the harmful effects of the proliferation of conventional arms throughout the world have reached the headlines—most recently in the Middle East.

The long-range effect of the arms sales program on our relations with our allies and with the Soviet Union and on the cause of peace in the world is, in my judgment, one of the most significant and one of the least discussed issues in our foreign policy. The Congress, particularly the Senate Committee on Foreign Relations, must give increasing attention to the desirability—and the very morality—of our arms distribution program.

4

Power
Through Pawns

The Central Intelligence Agency (CIA) is the most highly secret agency of the federal government. In recent years, it has become increasingly important in the formulation and execution of American foreign policy.

The dangers in an operation like that of the Central Intelligence Agency and in the extension of its powers are: first, that it can become a kind of law unto itself, operating independently even of the President of the United States; second, that operating under the direction of the President, it may perform acts which would otherwise not be authorized or approved, thus avoiding the constitutional limitation placed upon executive decisions and actions in the foreign policy field. Further, there is a danger that, sure of its objectives and its independence of action, it may become relatively indifferent to the methods and the means by which it seeks those objectives.

Defenders of the CIA assert that the President, with the help of his Cabinet and the National Security Council, controls and directs the CIA. Theoretically this is right. But the President is the nominal head of hundreds of agencies and cannot be kept fully informed at all times of the activities of an agency as large and as powerful as the CIA. Even if the CIA were fully under presidential control, the basic question of the right and duty of Congress to participate in decisions regarding the many Central Intelligence Agency activities would remain unanswered. The issue is not only one of executive control or of efficient administration of the CIA, but a fundamental one of the constitutional responsibility of the Congress. Over the years, some of the activities of the CIA have become known and accepted by some members of Congress, by readers of newspapers and of memoirs of former Presidents and their advisers.

There are three basic questions to be asked with reference to the Central Intelligence Agency:

What does the CIA do?

Does it do these things well or badly?

Are its actions properly authorized and controlled?

When first established, in 1947, under the direction of the National Security Council, the Central Intelligence Agency was authorized to advise the NSC in matters of intelligence activities: "to correlate and evaluate intelligence relating to the national security, and provide for the appropriate dissemination of such intelligence within the Government . . . ; to perform . . . such additional services of common concern as the National Security Council determines can be more effectively accomplished centrally"; and—most significant for its future development—the agency was authorized "to perform such other functions and duties related to intelligence affecting the national security as the National Security Council may from time to time direct."

There has been little complaint over the years about the intelligence-gathering and disseminating activities of the CIA. The agency has been praised especially for gathering information by U-2 reconnaissance flights and for the acquisition of Khrushchev's speech denouncing Stalin before it was edited for public consumption. It is alleged to have blundered in failing to anticipate the Chinese Communist entry into the Korean War, and it has been severely criticized for its faulty information—apart from its conduct of the operation—at the time of the Bay of Pigs invasion of Cuba in 1961. In this case, according to Kennedy Administration advisers, the CIA appears to have misread everything, from the strength of pro-Castro sentiment on the island, to the condition of Castro's air force, to the location of the coral reefs in the Bay of Pigs itself.*

It is the CIA's performance of "other functions and duties" that has raised most serious questions as to the operations of the agency. Because of the secrecy surrounding CIA activities, it is not possible to determine in full the validity of the criticisms or to prevent distortions or to dispel rumors.

The CIA is reported to have been involved in many incidents whose success or failure affected, and sometimes determined, the direction of U.S. policy in various parts of the world. It is not possible to document, in the accepted scholarly fashion, the responsibility of the CIA for specific actions or incidents. On the other hand, the CIA is not always free to answer false charges that are made against it. It must accept the brickbats with the laurels and probably, in some instances, one, when the other is deserved.

The New York *Times,* in a 1966 series of articles on the CIA, reported that during the early 1950's, CIA agents gathered remnants of defeated Chinese Nationalist armies in the jungles of northern Burma, supplied them with gold and arms, and encouraged them to raid Communist China. Although few raids occurred, the army became a costly and troublesome burden, particularly when it began to use CIA-supplied funds to go into the opium-smuggling business. The Burmese government was concerned because the Chinese troops were making common cause with rebel groups in Burma. By the time the CIA could rid itself of the force, Burma had renounced American aid and had threatened to quit the United Nations and move closer

---

* For extensive discussions of the Bay of Pigs, with particular emphasis on the CIA role, see Theodore C. Sorensen, *Kennedy* (New York, Harper & Row, 1965), pp. 294 ff., and Arthur M. Schlesinger, Jr., *A Thousand Days* (Boston, Houghton Mifflin, 1965), pp. 223–297.

to Peking. According to the *Times*, "some of the Nationalist Chinese are still in northern Burma . . . and still fomenting trouble . . . although they have not been supported by the CIA or any American agency for a decade."*

The U.S. Ambassador to Burma at the time said, "I had heard persistent reports that Americans were taking part when I was sent there. I found that hard to credit, but learned differently later.**

The CIA was also deeply involved in the politics of Laos and appears to have operated directly contrary to State Department policy. Arthur Schlesinger, Jr., former Presidential Assistant, and Roger Hilsman, former head of Intelligence in the State Department, have both testified to the difficulties that arose from U.S. support of Phoumi Nosavan, "the protégé of both the CIA and the Pentagon."†

Schlesinger indicates that by 1959 the State Department and the CIA were backing different Laotian factions and "the CIA station chief refused to follow the State Department policy or even tell the Ambassador his plans and intentions."‡ With the CIA building up Phoumi Nosavan, the situation finally reached the point where one of the factions was receiving U.S. military aid and the other U.S. economic aid. A Laotian leader complained to the American Ambassador about the various American agencies at work: "Since so many voices are heard, it is impossible to tell which has an authoritative ring."§

When the Kennedy Administration decided to reverse the earlier policy and support a neutral Laos,

* The New York *Times*, April 25, 1966. See also Frank N. Trager, *Burma, from Kingdom to Republic* (New York, Praeger, 1966), pp. 195–96, 231–32, 240, 428 (n 29).
** Quoted by Warren Unna, "CIA: Who Watches the Watchman?" *Harper's Magazine*, April 1958.
† *Hilsman*, p. 115.
‡ Schlesinger, pp. 325–26.
§ Quoted in Schlesinger, p. 326.

the CIA was still deeply committed to Phoumi Nosavan. Phoumi proved obstinate, for, in his experience, the CIA had always had the final word.* Finally, after two years of negotiations and threats, including denunciations of CIA activity in Laos in the British House of Commons, the neutralist regime of Prince Souvanna Phouma was restored. Meanwhile, millions of dollars of U.S. aid had been wasted and confusion spread about the aims of the United States in Laos.

In 1960, the CIA attempted to handle the bribing of the head of the government of Singapore to conceal a bungled American espionage effort. The bribe attempt, when it was revealed in 1965, was at first denied. Later, after Singapore's Prime Minister Lee Kuan Yew had made it public, the State Department acknowledged the existence of a letter of apology from Secretary of State Dean Rusk.

The CIA is also credited with having helped to oust the government of Premier Mohammed Mossadegh of Iran in 1953. History has not clearly demonstrated that this was the wisest policy. Its wisdom will probably never be decided one way or the other, but in any event, the authority of the CIA to take this action is open to question.

In 1954, fearful that President Jacobo Arbenz was leading Guatemala into communism, the CIA supported a movement to overthrow him.† Since that time, military regimes have succeeded one another in Guatemala, more or less violently, maneuvering erratically to stay in power amid worsening economic conditions, widely rumored graft and corruption, and growing political unrest. None of these successor gov-

---

* For an extensive discussion of events in Laos, including CIA activity, see Arthur J. Dommen, *Conflict in Laos* (New York, Praeger, 1964).

† Dwight D. Eisenhower, *Mandate for Change* (New York, Doubleday, 1963), pp. 504–12.

ernments has been progressive or even particularly stable. Efforts to build a progressive civilian government might have been encouraged years ago rather than delayed by support of right-wing military governments.

According to Roger Hilsman, President Kennedy considered that, in the light of things like the CIA's support of the 1958 rebellion in Indonesia, "Sukarno's frequently anti-American attitude was understandable." The Indonesians, Hilsman states, "had incontrovertible proof that the 1958 rebellion had received air drops of equipment from planes based in Malaya and the Philippines, and that the CIA was behind this support." The Indonesians had also shot down and captured an American pilot who was flying for the rebels; they had evidence that he was an employee of the CIA.* The pilot was finally released in 1962 at the insistence of the Kennedy Administration.

Surveillance of the Soviet Union through flights of U-2 reconnaissance aircraft was one of the CIA's most successful operations. Much useful information was collected. But the unfortunate incident of 1960, when a U-2 was brought down over the Soviet Union almost on the eve of the summit conference, is a clear demonstration of the manner in which clandestine activities carried out under a very general mandate from higher authority can seriously compromise our foreign policy objectives.

Each series of U-2 flights had been authorized by President Eisenhower, but it was never absolutely clear whether or not President Eisenhower was aware that there was to be a U-2 flight over the Soviet Union at that particular time. It appears that no one in a position of responsibility fully evaluated the possible consequences of a U-2 failure over Soviet terri-

* Hilsman, pp. 363, 364, 372.

tory. In any event, the CIA and the Joint Chiefs had assured the President that, if something went wrong, construction of the plane was such that it would disintegrate and that it would be impossible for the equipment or the pilot to fall into Soviet hands.[*]

According to the report of the Senate Foreign Relations Committee, which investigated the incident and its consequences:

> It appears that, although the President, the Vice President . . . and the appropriate Cabinet officers were knowledgeable of the program of flights, they were not knowledgeable of individual flights in advance, nor did they specifically approve of individual flights beyond a general approval within a given time span.[†]

Secretary of State Christian Herter told the Committee that the President had only general knowledge and that the National Security Council, which is supposed to be in direct and primary control of CIA activities, was aware only of the general program.[†] "It appears," the Foreign Relations Committee report continues, "that there was something very special about the May 1 flight, though the committee was unable to determine exactly what. . . . Both the President and the Secretary of State have said that the flight was mounted to secure very important information which might not be available later. Both the Secretary of State and the Director of the Central Intelligence Agency declined, for reasons of security, to tell the committee

---

[*] Dwight D. Eisenhower, *Waging Peace* (New York, Doubleday, 1965), p. 546.
[†] Senate Foreign Relations Committee, *Events Relating to the Summit Conference*, Senate Report No. 1761, 86th Cong., 2d. sess., p. 6.
[‡] *Hearings on Events Incident to the Summit Confernece*, 86th Cong., 2d. sess., 1960, pp. 63, 76.

what this information was." * On the basis of classified evidence presented to it in executive session, the Senate Foreign Relations Committee found no reason to believe that technical preparations for the flight were faulty or that the pilot was unreliable. The main question was the wisdom of the flight, and this the committee was unable to evaluate because the responsible officials refused to reveal the grounds on which it was determined that a risk to the summit conference and great embarrassment to the United States were justified. President Eisenhower was seriously embarrassed on the eve of his meeting with Chairman Khrushchev, the summit conference was wrecked, and U.S.-Soviet relations embittered for the remainder of the Eisenhower Administration.

No clear answers have been given to the question raised about the role of the Central Intelligence Agency in the Bay of Pigs invasion of Cuba. It is possible that the Central Intelligence Agency is being blamed for failures of the State Department or of other agencies of the government, although the testimony of those who were present when the decisions were made indicates heavy CIA responsibility. In any case, it is generally believed that the CIA made several erroneous judgments, including their assumption that large numbers of Cubans would support the invasion forces. Hilsman has pointed out that because of the CIA's concern for security, "men who had knowledge that could have contributed to the making of sounder judgments were excluded from making that contribution."† Some sources suggested the existence of CIA favoritism to the more conservative, or pro-Batista, elements among Cuban exiles being trained for the invasion. It seems quite clear that the CIA shares some of the guilt for the bungling of the invasion itself. And if the CIA

* Senate Report No. 1761, p. 7.
† Hilsman, p. 83.

did not actually deceive both President Kennedy and the leaders of the Cuban exiles, it seems evident that it failed to make clear to the President what to expect from the rebels.

Theodore Sorensen writes that after the invasion failed:

> It was clear to him [President Kennedy] . . . that he had in fact approved a plan bearing little resemblance to what he thought he had approved. . . . That so great a gap between concept and actuality should exist at so high a level on so dangerous a matter reflected a shocking number of errors in the whole decision-making process— errors which permitted bureaucratic momentum to govern instead of policy leadership."*

Arthur Schlesinger describes in detail the manner in which bureaucratic momentum and the "vested interest" of the CIA in the plan came to prevail. "By November 1960," he writes, "the CIA operation had taken on a life of its own. . . ." Kennedy saw the Cuban project as a contingency plan without realizing how contingency planning could "generate its own momentum and create its own reality."*†

The manner in which Allen Dulles, CIA Director, argued in favor of the plan illustrates how the contingency became the reality and how the CIA acted less as an analyst than as an advocate of its own project. "I stood right here at Ike's desk," Dulles told President Kennedy, "and told him I was certain our Guatamalan operation would succeed, and, Mr. President, the prospects for this plan are even better than they were for that one."‡ Dulles apparently suggested that, since the exile brigade had been created and trained and was anxious to proceed, failure to carry out

---

* Sorensen, p. 301–302.
*† Schlesinger, pp. 23, 233, 241.
‡ Quoted by Sorenson, p. 296.

the invasion would mean that the members of the brigade would scatter all over the United States and Latin America, exposing CIA operations and criticizing the United States for having let them down. Kennedy appears to have been impressed by this argument. "Contingency had thus become a reality;" reports Schlesinger, "having created the Brigade as an option, the CIA now presented its use against Cuba as a necessity."*

Of course, the ultimate responsibility for this invasion, as for all foreign policy, rests with the executive branch of the government, acting in consultation with the Congress.

But the CIA undoubtedly was very persuasive and influential. According to Senator J. William Fulbright, who was present at the meeting prior to the invasion with President Kennedy and others, the CIA Director actively promoted the project. "Allen Dulles was making a case for it," Fulbright told the Senate in July of 1966, "and was urging the President at that time to make a final decision . . . that would be a green light to proceed. I was there. I heard it."

The general evidence is that in addition to gathering and interpreting information, the CIA does play an important part in influencing foreign policy, and certainly has become an important operating arm of the executive branch in this area of government responsibility. President Harry Truman, during whose Administration the CIA was established, wrote in the Washington *Post* in 1963 that the original intention was to set up "a special organization charged with the collection of all intelligence reports from every available source," thus avoiding the previous practice under which intelligence reports tended to be slanted to conform to the positions of the various departments or

* Schlesinger, pp. 241, 242, 247.

agencies that collected intelligence. President Truman
continued:

> The most important thing about this move was
> to guard against the chance of intelligence being
> used to influence or to lead the President into un-
> wise decisions—and I thought it was necessary
> that the President do his own thinking and evalua-
> tion. . . .
>
> For some time I have been disturbed by the
> way CIA has been diverted from its original as-
> signment. It has become an operational and at
> times a policy-making arm of the Government.
> This has led to trouble and may have com-
> pounded our difficulties in several explosive areas.
>
> I never had any thought . . . when I set up the
> CIA that it would be injected into peacetime cloak
> and dagger operations. Some of the complications
> and embarrassment that I think we have experi-
> enced are in part attributable to the fact that this
> quiet intelligence arm of the President has been
> so removed from its intended role that it is being
> interpreted as a symbol of sinister and mysterious
> foreign intrigue—and a subject for cold war
> enemy propaganda. . . .
>
> I, therefore, would like to see the CIA . . . re-
> stored to its original assignment as the intelligence
> arm of the President . . . and its operational duties
> terminated. . . .

These words of President Truman indicate that
the CIA has taken on a role far beyond the one it
was intended to perform when it was established in
1947 by the National Security Act "for the purpose of
coordinating intelligence activities."

After the crisis of the Bay of Pigs, the Kennedy
Administration entertained several proposals to curb

CIA independence as well as to separate its intelligence gathering and evaluating from its operational functions. The situation as described by Arthur Schlesinger is revealing:

> Cuba and Laos had already provided the new administration with horrible examples of the readiness of CIA operatives in the field to go off on policies of their own. This was only the most spectacular expression of the steady growth of the CIA in the 1950's. The CIA's budget now exceeded State's by more than 50 percent (though it was less than half of that of the intelligence operations of the Defense Department). Its staff had doubled in a decade. . . . It had almost as many people under official cover overseas as State; in a number of embassies CIA officers outnumbered those from State in the political sections. Often the CIA station chief had been in the country longer than the ambassador, had more money at his disposal and exerted more influence. The CIA had its own political desks and military staffs, its own air force, even, on occasion, its own combat forces. . . . The coincidence that one Dulles brother was head of State and another the head of the CIA had resulted in practical independence for the Agency. . . .

While not an invisible government and while often taking a more liberal line than State, continues Schlesinger, "none the less it had acquired a power which, however beneficial its exercise often might be, blocked State Department control of foreign affairs."[*]

Several incidents occurred during 1966 to support the charge that in addition to its widespread overseas operations the Central Intelligence Agency is active,

[*] Schlesinger, pp. 427–28.

both in operations and as a propaganda instrument, in the United States. The lead article in the April 1966 issue of the quarterly *Foreign Affairs* described the Viet Cong in a manner that gave strong support to the Administration's charge that the National Liberation Front in South Vietnam is merely a creation and puppet of Hanoi. This article was presented as a piece of scholarly research by a disinterested observer. In reality the author was a full-time employee of the CIA, a fact which *Foreign Affairs* concealed from its readers. The same issue of *Foreign Affairs* contained an article on U.S. relations with Europe, written by a State Department official who was properly identified.

The Central Intelligence Agency's support of university projects also gives grave cause for concern. The extent to which the Michigan State University project in South Vietnam served as a cover for CIA operations will probably never be fully revealed. The April 1966 issue of *Ramparts* magazine charged that from 1955 to 1959, while operating a U.S. technical assistance program that trained police and other public officials for the Ngo Dinh Diem government, the university provided cover and support for CIA operations in South Vietnam. The connection between the CIA and the Michigan State project had been reported in 1965 in a little-noticed publication of the Center for the Study of Democratic Institutions of the Fund for the Republic, *How the United States Got Involved in Vietnam*. In April 1966, the MSU professor who had been in charge of the Vietnam project admitted the connection with the CIA to the New York *Times*, but the president of the university insisted that there was no proof that any CIA "agents" were involved. Without debating what might constitute an "agent," it seems evident that the university, whether with reluctance or enthusiasm, permitted itself to be involved in CIA operations or allowed the CIA to utilize university activities as a cover.

In early 1967, substantial revelations about the activities of the Central Intelligence Agency in the United States precipitated a widespread public and congressional debate over the methods and means the agency was using. On February 13, 1967, the National Student Association, the largest student organization in the country, acknowledged that for the previous fifteen years it had been subsidized by the Central Intelligence Agency. At one point, CIA had provided as much as 80 percent of the NSA budget; in addition, it was making the mortgage payments on the building that served as NSA headquarters in Washington.

The State Department, acknowledging that CIA had been contributing money to the student organization, defended the action as necessary to offset the influence in international student circles of heavily subsidized student groups from Communist countries. The Administration maintained that the CIA infiltration was perfectly legal because it was authorized by the National Security Council and, by implication, by the President.

The relationship between the CIA and the NSA was known to only a few of the top officers of the NSA each year. These officers negotiated for CIA funds directly with the agency, and the funds were transferred through a series of tax-exempt foundations and private individuals. Some of the foundations, many of whose names appeared in the press in subsequent days, were entirely CIA dummy organizations. They had no existence apart from a mailing address. Others had legitimate activities of their own, but had agreed to act as conduits for CIA funds, transferring them to the National Student Association or to other organizations to which the CIA was contributing.

Some of these foundations also passed CIA funds to labor unions, church groups, other student groups, educational groups, organizations with publishing and broadcasting affiliates, and other organizations that had

been used by the CIA over a period of years. Some of
the foundations that has served as CIA conduits admitted their role, but several groups receiving funds,
such as the American Newspaper Guild, stated that
they were unaware of the actual source of the funds
they had accepted.

While the primary purpose of the CIA infiltration
of these organizations appears to have been to work
through them abroad, CIA penetration of domestic
organizations raises serious questions.

First, there is the responsibility of the leaders of
those organizations to their constituencies. Many members of organizations identified as having been subsidized by the CIA admitted that they would not have
wished to be associated with the organizations had
they been aware of the relationship.

By requiring loyalty oaths whereby disclosure would
subject the officers involved to severe penalties, the
CIA was imposing on those officers a responsibility
which it claimed was greater and would, therefore,
erase their responsibility to the members of their organizations who believed them to be free agents.

Second, the subsidization by the CIA of organizations which disseminate information within the United
States by publishing books and magazines, or by operating broadcasting facilities, raises the question of
the right of citizens to be reasonably secure against
their own government's propaganda. It is generally
accepted that public funds should not be used in the
United States to indoctrinate the people nor to help the
government tone down citizen criticism of government
policies. There was evidence that CIA influence in
some of these organizations was used to moderate
criticism of such Administration policies as the bombing of North Vietnam.

The third major problem raised by the CIA's domestic operations relates to basic principles and processes in a free society. One of the dangers inherent in

a secret agency is that of the "Inner Ring," whose pitfalls and temptations have been best described by C. S. Lewis in his essay entitled *The Inner Ring*. "I am not going to say," he wrote, "that the existence of the Inner Ring is an evil. . . . The desire which draws us into Inner Rings is another matter. A thing can be morally neutral and yet the desire for that thing may be dangerous. . . . This desire is one of the great permanent mainsprings of human action. . . . Of all passions the passion for the Inner Ring is most skillful in making a man who is not yet a very bad man do very bad things."

When this strong and deep human drive is legalized, given public function, it becomes, possibly, even more potent.

The Inner Ring of a secret agency is privileged. It becomes a kind of secular order of the elect. Full individual choice and responsibility are limited to oath of obligation to the agency. Individual conscience is eased in the general certainty of the over-all good of the object being pursued.

The anonymity of the service becomes a kind of habit, a rejection of the world of name and credit and recognition. In the end, the process may become the end, and doing the wrong things for the right reasons becomes increasingly easy. With this development may also come the temptation of other agencies to escape responsibilities and accountability by transferring more and more to the special agency that has immunity.

A secret agency must be most carefully watched during a cold war under conditions of uncertainty and anxiety. Since the danger is undefined, it may be everywhere; counteraction, therefore, it may be argued, also must be unlimited.

Kafka comes very close to describing the mood and motivation in *The Burrow*, his story of an animal's anxiety and efforts to preserve and protect his possessions and his burrow by building mazes, moats, new tunnels, chambers—all manner of defenses and deceit. "Completely to trust someone outside the burrow when you are inside the burrow, that is in a different world, that, it seems to me, is impossible," writes Kafka. "Now the truth of the matter—and one has no eye for that in times of great peril, and only by a great effort even in times when danger is threatening— is that in reality the burrow does provide a considerable degree of security, but by no means enough, for is one ever free from anxieties inside it?"

Under this drive of insecurity, all persons and institutions may become instruments. The secret security agents move from government to business, then to the use of academic organizations and scholars and even students, unmindful of what they are doing or indifferent to the consequences of their actions.

Henry Steele Commager stated the pure case before the Senate Foreign Relations Committee on February 20, 1967, when he said:

> The activities of the CIA in the various realms which have been called to our attention of late violate two of the great Kantian categorical imperatives: the first is never use any human being as a means but always as an end; and the second is so to conduct yourself that you might generalize your every action into a universal rule.
>
> The danger, as I see it, in what the CIA is doing in subsidizing the press, subsidizing student and labor and religious organizations, and various other activities, is that it substitutes the immediate advantage for the long run disadvantage; that it uses great things like scholarship, science, the community of learning, truth, for immediate purposes, which it doubtless thinks are worthy, but which, in the long run, are not to be compared with the larger purposes of learning, scholarship, literature,

art, and truth. And the reason that they are not to be compared in the long run is that that is what the short-run purposes are about.

The reason we are trying to win the contest with communism is precisely because we want the triumph of the open mind, the triumph of the unimpeded investigation of every scientific, every moral and philosophical question, and if we corrupt that process at the very outset, we may win the contest with communism and lose the purposes for which we are contesting.

If we expose the great processes of the academy —the processes of the search for truth at whatever point, smaller things like student organizations, larger things like scholarly undertakings—if we begin to corrupt those, we have sacrificed something irrevocable, something which existed long before there were any nations and which will, I trust, exist long after our current notion of nations has been transformed.

We will expose to danger and, perhaps, to destruction, the search for truth through those delicate, those infinitely delicate, processes of intellectual freedom built up century after century.

Without intellectual freedom, absolute, uncontaminated and beyond suspicion, we cannot achieve the ends which our society is dedicated to achieving. This is ultimately why the activities of the CIA, whatever their immediate and short-term advantages may be, are fraught with very grave danger.

As a result of the disclosure of CIA infiltration of the National Student Association and other domestic institutions, President Johnson ordered a review by a Cabinet-level committee of the relationship between government agencies, notably the CIA, and educational and private voluntary organizations which operate abroad.

The report of the Cabinet-level committee, made public at the end of March 1967, recommended: first, "it should be the policy of the United States Government that no Federal agency shall provide any covert financial assistance or support, direct or indirect, to any of the nation's educational or private voluntary organizations"; and second, "the Government should promptly develop and establish a public-private mechanism to provide public funds openly for overseas activities or organizations which are adjudged deserving, in the national interest, of public support."

Throughout the years of CIA's existence, members of the Congress have made repeated attempts to establish greater congressional control over, or review of, its activities. These attempts have not met with success; the CIA has friends on Capitol Hill, among them powerful members of the Senate and House "Defense Establishment." In the twenty-year period since the establishment of the agency, only two of the actions relating to the CIA proposed in the Senate have ever been reported out of committee. The first was the 1956 proposal by Senator Mike Mansfield for the establishment of a Joint Committee on Central Intelligence. The Mansfield proposal was defeated on the floor of the Senate on April 11, 1956.

The controversy was again brought to a head in the Senate in 1966. This time the issue was whether or not we who were members of the Senate Foreign Relations Committee should be given the same kind of information with reference to the activities of the Central Intelligence Agency as is given to certain members of the Armed Services Committee and of the Appropriations Committee of the Senate, who have for the past ten years or so acted as a kind of informal subcommittee on the CIA.

On July 14, 1966, the Senate Foreign Relations Committee reported an original resolution providing for the creation of a Committee on Intelligence Operations to become effective at the beginning of the 90th Congress. The resolution provided for a nine-member committee, composed of three members each from the Appropriations, Armed Services, and Foreign Relations committees of the Senate. The Committee on Intelligence Operations would have been empowered to keep itself informed of all activities in the field of foreign intelligence. The practical effect of the resolution would have been simply to add three members of the Foreign Relations Committee to the existing informal Central Intelligence Agency subcommittee.

At stake in the dispute over proper supervision of the CIA is nothing less than the constitutional responsibility of the Senate to "advise and consent" to the foreign policy of the United States. This responsibility is vested principally in the Committee on Foreign Relations, as an instrument of the Senate. The standing rules of the Senate list among other areas of jurisdiction for that committee "relations of the United States with foreign nations generally" and "intervention abroad and declarations of war." According to the committee report, "As a matter of principle, the Committee on Foreign Relations believes selected members should be in a position to receive information regarding Central Intelligence Agency activities which influence our foreign relations with other countries and which could mean the difference between war and peace."

The debate on the resolution was held in closed session of the Senate and was generally irrelevant to the real issue, which is the extent to which the Central Intelligence Agency is involved not only in the execution of foreign policy, but directly and indirectly in the formulation of such policy, and particularly the issue of whether or not the Foreign Relations Committee should have greater jurisdiction over the operation of this agency and be more fully informed as to its function and role.

During the debate, it was charged that if the resolution were passed it would imply a judgment of dereliction against those members of the Senate who currently act as "watchdogs" of the CIA. Such a judgment was certainly not the intention of the members of the Senate who supported the resolution. If any charge of dereliction could have been made, it might have been made against the Foreign Relations Committee had it not sought to provide itself with the information it requires in order to fulfill its responsibility to the Senate.

Second, it was argued that individuals who serve as sources of information for the Central Intelligence Agency or who are agents in that organization would be compromised and that even their lives might be threatened if members of the Foreign Relations Committee were permitted to exercise this jurisdiction. It was even suggested that the very discussion of the Central Intelligence Agency in the Senate might imperil lives.

Generally, these charges were irrelevant. There was nothing in the resolution to suggest that members of the Foreign Relations Committee were concerned with knowing the identity of individuals who might serve the Central Intelligence Agency or that they were concerned with any kind of supervision of its day-by-day operations.

Further, it was suggested rather strongly that some members of the Senate could not be trusted with information that involved the national security of the United States. This charge, of course, was never substantiated or personalized. If it was the judgment of the Senate that the membership of the Foreign Relations Committee was unreliable, then consideration could have been given to changing that membership.

Finally, it was argued that the number of persons with access to information about any secret agency ought to be limited since, as the number grew, the possibility of leaks of information increased. Certainly this is a generalization that could not be challenged. Carried to its logical end, however, it would mean that no member of the Congress should be trusted with any kind of responsibility for scrutiny of any of the agencies of the federal government in whose operation secrecy is necessary or defensible.

Yet, the argument loses its force when we examine the present situation. In the Senate, the CIA subcommittee had a potential membership of nine during the 89th Congress, five members from the Armed Services Committee and four from the Appropriations Committee. Actually, during the 89th Congress only seven Senators were serving because of overlapping membership. Then, at the beginning of the 90th Congress, the membership went up to nine—although this time there were six Senators from Armed Services and three from Appropriations.

In the House, supervision of the CIA is carried out by a subcommittee of the Armed Services Committee, composed of the eleven ranking members of that committee. The House Appropriations Committee also has responsibility for scrutinizing the CIA, but that committee has always declined to state (1) who the members are who perform this function, (2) how many members are involved, (3) how they are selected, and (4) whether a subcommittee exists. It seems unlikely that all fifty members of the House Appropriations Committee are privy to the secrets of the Central Intelligence Agency. It is possible, but we do not know.

Although the resolution to establish a Committee on Intelligence Operations failed to win Senate approval during the 89th Congress, much of its essential purpose was achieved. In January 1967, the chairman of the

Senate CIA subcommittee invited three members of the Foreign Relations Committee, its Chairman Senator Fulbright, its ranking minority member Senator Bourke Hickenlooper, and its third ranking majority member Senator Mansfield, to be present at all meetings of the subcommittee, including those dealing with appropriations. The Foreign Relations members, however, are not considered actual "members" of the CIA subcommittee and it is, as yet, not clear what their role will be.

While a formal procedure for congressional supervision of the Central Intelligence Agency established by action of the Senate would be preferable, the informal invitation at least provides selected members of the Foreign Relations Committee with information which can assist them in carrying out their constitutional responsibilities.

From the first twenty years of experience with the Central Intelligence Agency, and particularly from the recent disclosures about its domestic activities, it should be clear to the American people that the activities of this secret agency of the executive branch, the CIA, are in need of continuous supervision by the Congress.

5

Rhetoric or Reality
in Latin America

President Eduardo Frei of Chile, in an article in *Foreign Affairs* of April 1967, sets forth in forceful terms the challenge of Latin America today.

> The Latin American revolution, as a force for rapid and substantial change, has been germinating for the last decade; it is now a permanent and dynamic torrent which is weakening the political and social institutions of the continent. The form taken by this drastic change will depend on the time which elapses before the forces of revolution are finally released. The greater the delay, the greater will be the accumulated pressure and the greater the violence of the eventual explosion.

Through the Alliance for Progress, the United States is pledged to respond to that challenge, to assist the forces for change.

But if the United States is to meet its historical obligations to the Latin American nations, if we are to safeguard our vital interests in the hemisphere, if we are to fulfill the promise of the Alliance, we must revise our present policies. We must close the gap between myth and reality in our Latin American policy.

The Alliance for Progress began with promise, but the promise has been blurred, particularly by our military intervention in the Dominican Republic in 1965. Many Latin Americans have come to regard the Alliance with cynicism. They see the disparity between reality and rhetoric. President Johnson, in the 1967 foreign aid bill, requested only $624 million for economic aid to the area. The Administration proposed to add to this an average of $300 million per year to help ease the problems which will arise in the formation of the common market to which the Latin American nations agreed at Punta del Este in April 1967.

At the same time, Latin America, taken as a whole, has:

—the highest rate of population growth in the world, 2.9 percent per year, far outstripping her economic growth;

—low living standards and inadequate and ill-distributed purchasing power, land, and income;

—growing gaps in income and living standards between rural and urban areas;

—rapid migration of population to the cities, which has led to more slums, unemployment, and unrest;

—inadequate and inflexible credit and market systems, leading to exploitation, inflation, and decreasing returns to the farmer;

—inadequate education and rigid hierarchical social structures which cut off opportunity for those few who do manage to get an education. (The area has an average literacy of 68 percent, but this is misleading, for it ranges from highs of 91 percent in Argentina and Uruguay to 10 percent in Haiti—and this is an area with at least two universities, Lima and Mexico, that are a century older than Harvard.)

In addition to these difficulties, the Latin American problem is compounded by remnants of feudalism which stifle change, initiative, confidence, and even hope. A lack of confidence in the future and a lack of trust and communication between social groups have led to social and economic isolation.

Traditionally Latin America has had a close political and economic identification with the United States. History, proximity, security, and justice have all played a role in the development of obligations to Latin America, obligations that are at the root of the special relationship which exists today and which must be recognized.

This relationship is based on considerations of strategy and defense, on a certain measure of shared ideology, and on the enormous leverage exerted by the great economic and cultural strength of the United States relative to Latin America. We also share with the rest of the hemisphere a common tradition of Western civilization. Latin America had an extended history of European colonialism and a long and varied experience with European custom, tradition, and thought.

The desire to establish and enforce an exclusively American hemisphere, politically and militarily, has been a consistent feature of United States foreign policy throughout our history. In 1811 the Congress, in secret session, passed a resolution concerning Florida, then under weak Spanish control, whose key phrase was that the United States "cannot, without serious inquietude, see any part of the said territory [Florida] pass into the hands of any foreign power." This was the first formulation of the idea of an exclusively American sphere in the New World and was the germ of the Monroe Doctrine, enunciated twelve years later.

At that time, President James Monroe determined to take an independent stand against any European intervention to restore Spanish rule to the recently independent American nations, rejected a British proposal for joint action in favor of a unilateral declaration. The Monroe Doctrine was formally proclaimed to the world in the President's message to the Congress on December 2, 1823. In its essential paragraph, Monroe stated:

.With the existing Colonies or dependencies of any European power, we have not interfered, and shall not interfere. But with the Governments who have declared their Independence, and maintained it, and whose Independence we have, on great consideration, and on just principles, acknowledged, we could not view any interposition for the purpose of oppressing them, or controuling [sic] in any other manner, their destiny, by any European power, in any other light, than as the manifestation of an unfriendly disposition towards the United States.

Thus we proclaimed an American doctrine for the Western Hemisphere which even today is invoked to protect the hemisphere against what is conceived to be the new menace: Communist-inspired wars of national liberation.

The United States was sympathetic to the South American independence efforts of the nineteenth century for both philosophical and practical reasons: first, because to a large extent, the nations of South America were basing their struggles for freedom on the ideals of the American revolution—many adopted constitutions patterned on our own; second, because there was sympathy for those who wished to throw off the yoke of European rule as we ourselves had thrown it off; third, because trade with the areas to the south of our borders was becoming increasingly important to us; fourth, because for strategic reasons, the United States welcomed the weakening of European influence in the hemisphere and was interested in seeing it driven out entirely.

Another fact bearing on our policy, one that has left a legacy of problems, was construction of the Panama Canal. The desire of the United States to see a canal built was understandable. It was prompted by the problems arising from our westward expansion and the requirement for a quick sea route from coast to coast. While there is no direct evidence that high officials of the U.S. government actually conspired with those officials of the Panama Canal Company who were behind the Panamanian insurrection against the government of Colombia in 1903, the United States clearly took full advantage of the situation. President Theodore Roosevelt ordered U.S. warships to prevent the landing of Colombian troops sent to put down the rebellion; in later years, Roosevelt claimed, "I took Panama."

The treaty of 1903 between the United States and the new Republic of Panama, which came into being as the result of the rebellion, gave the United States the right to build the canal, to fortify it, and to possess the ten-mile-wide Canal Zone "as if it were sovereign." Other articles of the treaty gave the United States the right to take land in Panama by eminent domain and to intervene to maintain and protect the canal; in effect, the treaty made Panama an American protectorate, a situation which continued until 1939.

With increasing tensions in Panama in recent years, culminating in the riots and temporary break in relations between the United States and Panama in 1964, it has become clear that alteration in the status of the Canal Zone will be necessary to insure continued good relations with the Republic of Panama.

Out of the necessity to secure the Canal and its approaches, the United States exercised a police power in the Caribbean from the early years of the twentieth century until shortly before World War II. We intervened in the Caribbean countries both to restore order to their finances and to build up their military forces to maintain political stability.

Thus, in 1916, President Woodrow Wilson began an armed intervention in the Dominican Republic which lasted until 1924; the Marines intervened in Haiti from 1915 until 1934 and in Nicaragua from 1912 until 1933. The Platt Amendment to the U.S. Army appropriations bill of 1901, giving us the right to intervene in Cuba, was embodied both in a treaty (May 22, 1903) and in the Cuban constitution itself. In 1934 a new treaty abolished the Platt Amendment, but we retained our naval base at Guantanamo, and U.S. forces remain in Cuba at that base today.

The United States bombardment and temporary occupation of the Mexican port city of Vera Cruz in 1914 was an intervention of a different character. It was brought about by a refusal by the Mexicans to salute the American flag.

By the early 1930's, with America strong and Europe absorbed in its own problems, security seemed assured, and the way was open for a change of policy toward Latin America. From the first inaugural address of President Franklin D. Roosevelt came a felicitous phrase: the Good Neighbor Policy. On March 4, 1933, without specifically mentioning Latin America, Roosevelt declared:

> In the field of world policy I would dedicate this Nation to the policy of a good neighbor—the neighbor who resolutely respects himself and, because he does so, respects the rights of others— the neighbor who respects his obligations and respects the sanctity of his agreements in and with a world of neighbors.

In putting into practice the Good Neighbor Policy, Roosevelt was advancing a policy that had been developing during the Coolidge and Hoover Administrations. Roosevelt, however, added the crucial principle, the acceptance of nonintervention in the affairs of the nations of Latin America, as embodied in the convention adopted at Montevideo in 1933. The Good Neighbor Policy was an evolutionary rather than a revolutionary change in our policy; yet it illustrates the importance of expressing such attitudes in international relations, for to the Latins it symbolized a new era.

The Charter of the Organization of American States, signed at Bogota in 1948, formally commits the United States and all the American states to the principle of non-intervention. It provides:

> No State or group of States has the right to intervene, directly or indirectly, for any reason whatever, in the internal or external affairs of any other State. The foregoing principle prohibits not only armed force but also any other form of interference or attempted threat against the personality of the State or against its political, economic, and cultural elements. (Art. XV)

and

> The Territory of a State is inviolable; it may not be the object, even temporarily, of military occupation or of other measures of force taken by another State, directly or indirectly, on any grounds whatever. (Art. XVII)

The only exception to these prohibitions is that which provides for *collective* action taken under the Rio Treaty, the Inter-American Treaty of Reciprocal Assistance.

Under the Eisenhower Administration, Latin America was not an area of primary concern. John Foster Dulles was content to ask for a policy which would be "imaginative, but which wouldn't cost any money." Intervention, although formally eschewed, was practiced in a limited and covert manner by U.S. assistance in the overthrow of President Arbenz of Guatemala in 1954.

During the 1950's, our Military Assistance Program in Latin America was used to reinforce and bolster the *status quo*. Our economic assistance, too, was dedicated to keeping the area politically and economically stable. This emphasis on collective security and nonintervention had the effect of stabilizing the power of dictators.

By 1960, however, the Castro revolution in Cuba and other considerations convinced the United States that a new approach was required. With the advent of the Kennedy Administration, despite the ill-fated Bay of Pigs adventure, a new policy came into being. The decision was one of not trying to oppose all revolution, but rather of attempting to guide the revolutionary forces into moderate, non-Communist channels.

The Alliance for Progress, inaugurated in 1961, sought to change feudalistic land-holding patterns, to reduce poverty and social injustice, and to improve education.

The Alliance was the high watermark in our recent Latin American relations. Under its terms, the American republics, with aid from the United States, agreed to work together for the social and economic development of the region and promised to carry out a series of reforms, particularly in the fields of agriculture, tax, and fiscal administration.

The Kennedy Administration also applied limited political pressures in favor of democratic forces. In the Dominican Republic in 1961, in Peru in 1962, and in Haiti, Honduras, and the Dominican Republic again in 1963, nonrecognition, along with the suspension of economic and military assistance, were used against governments that had assumed power by nonconstitutional means. Further, in the Dominican Republic the United States used diplomatic, economic, and even military pressure (the stationing of warships off the coast) to discourage the return of a rightist dictatorship.

In recent years, and particularly since 1965, our Latin American policy has returned to one in which the emphasis is on stability. Intervention in the Dominican Republic in 1965 was justified on the basis of a supposedly imminent Communist take-over.

In San Diego, on October 12, 1965, Thomas Mann, former Undersecretary of State for Economic Affairs and chief Administration spokesman on Latin American policy at the time of the Dominican intervention, reiterated the belief that "nonintervention is a keystone of the structure of the inter-American system." This was not a new policy position; the novelty was in his interpretation of the terms. Nonintervention today, he insisted, requires that the United States refrain from any action or attitude that might be construed as "support" even for democratic forces or political parties of the non-Communist left. Such support, he maintained, would be intervention. The landing of U.S. troops in the Dominican Republic in April 1965, however, was not intervention by his interpretation, because it was a "response" to the "intervention" of Communist subversion. Thus, Mann was able not only to justify our failure to respond to calls for assistance and mediation by the moderates and the constitutionalist forces during the Dominican revolt in 1965, but also to justify our favorable response to the request for support by a military junta in the Dominican Republic a few days later.

United States intervention in the Dominican Republic raised many issues. It called into question some of the basic precepts of our foreign policy. Because this intervention was contrary to U.S. policy as it was generally understood and accepted in Latin America, our willingness to honor any of our treaty obligations was questioned.

Until the Dominican intervention, we seemed to be making progress in quieting fears of the Colossus of the North. We had entered into the Rio Treaty and signed the Charter of the OAS with its nonintervention pledge. Yet the OAS was brought into the picture in the Dominican Republic only after the fact and after U.S. troops had already landed.

Generalizations about Latin America are always dangerous. It is true, however, that for historical reasons the military has traditionally been a powerful force in Latin political life, although in some countries other elements of the society have developed sufficiently to provide a counterweight to its power.

Military elements may be so fundamental a feature of Latin American political life and so closely woven into the social fabric that it may be impossible to expect a real separation of the military from politics for a long time to come. In these cases, concentrating on improving the military may be the most prudent course. If an army can be professionalized and neutralized as a political force, it can become a support for democracy.

The Dominican Republic is a special case in that our intervention, as well as our previous neglect, have imposed special obligations. About 70 percent of the country is rural; there is no strong middle class; the rate of literacy is only about 50 percent.

Unless some progress can be made toward developing a more rational economic structure, it is unlikely that free institutions will be able to survive, and we will again be faced with a choice between a military and a Communist threat.

The Dominican Republic shares a major economic problem with most of Latin America, an inability to earn sufficient foreign exchange to finance development. It is a rich country of considerable potential, but generations of neglect by the ruling oligarchy have left it stagnant. It is dependent for foreign exchange largely on one commodity, sugar, which accounted for 53 percent of all export earnings in 1964. More than 80 percent of the annual production of approximately one million tons is exported. While diversification of agriculture is desirable, even an active effort in this direction cannot make its impact felt for several years.

If the United States were willing to permit a significant increase in the amount of Dominican sugar coming into this country, a substantial rise in Dominican export earnings could be expected. Unless we are willing to do something about sugar, little else we can do makes immediate economic sense.

Both the United States Congress and the Administration have failed to respond to the vital need of developing countries for foreign exchange derived from the sale of primary commodities. In 1965, the Congress allocated a quota of about 433,000 tons of sugar to countries outside the Western Hemisphere. Some of these countries are not even trade-deficit nations. Some of them are developing countries which already enjoy special trade arrangements with their former mother countries.

Congress allocated a quota of about 341,000 tons of sugar to the Dominican Republic for each of the five years following 1965. In my judgment this is most inadequate. I see no reason why we should not give the Dominican Republic a quota of 800,000 tons, the equivalent of its entire sugar export.

In addition to the need for a market, the Dominican sugar industry, of which the government-controlled sugar corporation accounts for 60 percent of production, is plagued with inefficiency and high production costs. Important improvements can be made through the application of more advanced agricultural and refinery techniques and the transfer of the industry to nongovernmental management and ownership. A start has been made in reorganizing the mills, and five thousand excess workers have been dismissed. Obviously, ways must be devised to absorb these displaced workers in other sectors of the economy.

Similar problems exist in the rest of Dominican industry. After the overthrow of Trujillo, the Dominican government nationalized the vast interests held by the Trujillo family and its associates. They had owned some 35 percent of all arable land in the country, over 60 percent of the sugar production, a large portion of the remaining exportable agricultural production, and eighty-seven industrial and commercial enterprises, some of which were partially owned by the state. The former Trujillo-owned industries, except for the sugar industry, are now owned and managed by the government-controlled Corporation for State Enterprises.

Taking into account commercial and agricultural property, it is estimated that about one-half of the Dominican economy is state owned, primarily as a result of nationalization of the Trujillo interests. The public agencies holding title to the former Trujillo interests may administer them in the public interest, or they may be permitted to sell them to private owners.

The latter change would have many advantages. It would return to the people that which was taken from them, and it would give them a sense of sharing in the future development of their country. The state holdings would be broken up and, as private industries run for the profit of the stockholders, could be operated more efficiently and responsibly. The companies would be taxable, and they would be able to borrow against their assets, thus giving an important boost to the economy.

As far as United States assistance is concerned, the Alliance and the substantial efforts made since the Dominican intervention have helped. But we need to ask: Is it enough?

Each country in Latin America calls for special attention. At the same time there is need for response within the context of larger organizations.

One of the most useful things the United States

might do for the future of our relations with Latin America is agree to a reform of the Organization of American States along lines generally acceptable to the Latin Americans and, indeed, very much desired by them.

Despite the tone of speeches by United States officials, Washington's stress has been on the peacekeeping functions of the OAS while Latin American leaders have stressed the economic and social functions of the organization.

Latin Americans have been calling for reform of the OAS for years, but Washington failed to respond until the Dominican crisis of 1965 forced our hand. "Out of the Dominican crucible," President Johnson declared, "the twenty American nations must now forge a stronger shield against disaster."

Washington's idea of the stronger shield was an inter-American force to deal with future situations like the Dominican. But this idea has been largely unacceptable to the progressive Latin American states. Washington may continue to press for an inter-American force, but it appears unlikely that reform of the OAS will ever come on that basis alone. There is no agreement between the United States and its American allies on the purpose for which such a force would be used. There would always be fear that the United States might use this military power to suppress democratic movements in the interest of "stability." Few states of Central and South America see it as being in their interest to cooperate in the creation of a permanent military force staffed largely by Latin American troops but armed and financed largely by the United States. Their fear is that the force would really be created to serve U.S. interests, that the U.S. would control it, and that we would determine where and when it was to be used. Many Latin Americans question our ability to understand or sympathize with movements of radical reform, and they sometimes doubt the adequacy of the information upon which our policy decisions, such as the Dominican decision, are based. They believe that on the issues of peacekeeping and inter-American security, the will and power of the United States are going to prevail no matter what structure of collective decision might be patched together.

Because it is unlikely that an OAS peacekeeping role can be developed until a more equitable power relationship between the United States and Latin America evolves, it might be desirable for the United Nations to take a more active role than it has in the past in the security problems of the hemisphere. Many of the problems are somewhat similar to those which the United Nations has handled in other areas.

The difference in outlook between the United States and the other American states is explained by President Frei of Chile, quoted in an article in the *New Leader,* October 10, 1966:

> In the United States, Communism is a problem of power, a problem of relative military and economic strength among the U.S., Russia and China. But in Latin America Communism is an internal, not a foreign, problem. Communism is a danger to Latin America because it has found roots in the soil here. It thrives with or without Castro because he is not the important element. The strength of Communism in Latin America is born and resides in the masses, among peasants and marginal people without land, slum dwellers and workers with low salaries—in other words, in the poverty and more than that in the misery of the people. They seek in Communism a way to change their lives and that is what Communism and sometimes Communism alone offers them.
>
> Second, Communism also has great ideological appeal. The young people in Latin America are

restless and searching for answers to our problems. They look to politics to supply some of these answers. Thus in Latin America Communism is also a problem of philosophy, of ideas. It is not a police problem to be dealt with by repression. The first weapon against Communism in Latin America is economic development and social justice—social justice in particular because many times economic development favors only a small group. It is very important for the United States to understand this.

Latin American leaders have attempted to keep the focus of OAS reform pressure on economic and social questions. Many want to convert the OAS into a true economic and social instrument and to incorporate into its charter the basic principles of the Alliance for Progress.

The United States, on the other hand, is reluctant to commit itself by treaty and to allow too much authority over inter-American economic affairs and control of Alliance funds to be vested in a body in which the United States is outnumbered by nineteen votes to one.

But under the Marshall Plan for European recovery we did not commit ourselves by treaty. We were not a member of the Organization for European Economic Cooperation which planned the recovery of Europe. The United States should consider a similar procedure and relationship with the Latin American countries. There is little real hope for reform of the OAS and for making it a truly effective instrument of hemisphere cooperation unless the United States is willing to give up some of the political leverage we gain by keeping tight control over determining who gets what in the Alliance. The Alliance can never be a truly cooperative effort as long as it continues to operate as one supplier and nineteen receivers. A cooperative venture, in which the Latin Americans themselves would determine which countries would receive which funds, would put the burden of responsibility on the Latin Americans to move to integrate their economies. It would also give them valuable experience in joint planning.

The problems of Latin America are very great, and the obligation of the United States to help is clear. The success of the Alliance and the future of the OAS will depend on more than the support of the United States. It will also depend on the will of the Latin countries to make the difficult political decisions, the hard choices and sacrifices, necessary for implementing the programs. And, perhaps more significantly, it will depend on the will of the United States to make the difficult decisions which have long been needed, decisions which affect the essentials of our trade relations with Latin America.

President Carlos Lleras Restrepo of Colombia has stated the problem plainly, "Economic integration between a group of poor countries is not enough to assure our growth at a satisfactory rate. We need greater access to the markets of the wealthier countries." *

Money is not enough. What more is needed? I would suggest the following as a basis for United States policy: (1) Increased access to our markets, with the possibility of import concessions to companies that will give substantial investment guarantees to the Latin American countries. (2) Reduction or elimination of tariff barriers. In 1965 we concluded with the Canadian government a tariff-reduction agreement involving automotive products, which is expected to benefit the industry on both sides of the border. This special arrangement was justified by the Administration on the basis of our special relationship with Canada. Our relationships with the Latin American

---

* The New York *Times*, August 25, 1966.

countries generally are no less extraordinary. (3) A better market at stable prices for Latin American tropical products such as sugar, cotton, bananas, and coffee. The primary products of the Latin countries, which are their chief source of foreign exchange earnings, are, to a considerable extent, frozen out of the European market by the preferences European countries grant to developing nations that were formerly their colonies.

Our policy toward Latin America today is ambivalent and somewhat contradictory. We offer aid, but we are unwilling to make the profound revisions in our trade policies without which Latin America will be unable to make significant progress toward development.

We talk of nonintervention and act in violation of treaty commitments as in the Dominican intervention in 1965. We cannot have it both ways.

It is time for the United States to demonstrate by concrete action the special relationship between the American nations and our special concern for the nations of Central and South America.

6

Conflicts or Cooperation in Europe

Because of World War II and the political instability of Europe in the years after the war, Russia was able to achieve, in great measure, her traditional aims: the establishment of satellite states on her western frontier and the fragmentation of German power. Weakness in Western Europe, compounded by the existence of large Communist parties in France and Italy, created a danger that communism, if not Russia, might become master of Europe.

The North Atlantic Treaty and the Marshall Plan were appropriate responses to that challenge. Europe did not fall under Russian or Communist domination. Political stability returned to Europe, and her war-devastated economies were rebuilt under our protection and with our assistance.

The year 1966 marked the formal end of an era, an era which had begun at the end of World War II. It was the year of truth in United States-European relationships. It was the year in which President de Gaulle formally took French troops out of NATO. It was the year in which the United States removed its military establishment from French soil. It was the year that saw the displacement in Germany of the Christian Democratic Union, which had controlled the government since the formation of the Federal Republic in 1949.

No one of these events should have come as a complete surprise, nor is any one of them disastrous to common United States-European objectives. On the contrary, the United States and Europe are doing well in the pursuit of common objectives in Europe largely because of the success of the Marshall Plan and the early commitment under NATO and because of the inherent strength of the culture and traditions of the United States and Western Europe. As Edmund Burke wrote, "Men are not tied to one another by paper and seals. They are led to associate by resemblances, by conformities, by sympathies. It is with nations as with individuals. Nothing is so strong a tie of amity between nation and nation as correspondence in laws, customs, manners, and habits of life. They are obligations written in the heart."

The European countries in NATO have never met their original armed force goals despite constant United States pressure. If they had, NATO would be saddled with a much larger armed force, which the countries concerned would probably have had difficulty financing. The result would undoubtedly have been an increased financial burden on the United States.

The European countries have refused to follow the United States in increasing the size and role of NATO. If they had, there would have been increased emphasis on continuing the cold war rather than ending it and on maintaining a belligerent posture toward the European Communist world.

As a matter of fact, the situation in Europe is better because some of our policies failed and because others were never adopted.

The United States very early became an advocate of Germany's return as a major force on the European scene and of German rearmament and integration into a United States-European community. The United States fostered the idea of a European Defense Community, providing for a European army into which German units would be integrated. In 1953, Washington asserted that the establishment of the EDC was a condition for future United States commitments of military aid for the defense of Europe. The Congress in 1953 authorized the President to hold up as much as one billion dollars in military assistance for Europe if

the Europeans did not agree to the EDC. In presenting
the conference report on the Mutual Security bill to
the House of Representatives in July 1953, the bill's
manager, Congressman John Vorys, stated:

> We have a long-time reliable interest in Euro-
> pean unification. This must take place or else we
> reserve the right to do some rethinking based on
> presidential recommendations. This is an "or else"
> policy statement.

The idea of EDC "or else" was reinforced by Secretary Dulles' famous statement that the United States
would undertake an "agonizing reappraisal" of our
policy toward Europe if the Europeans did not go
along with our wishes in the matter of EDC.

Europe failed to accept the European Defense Community despite strong United States urging. If it had
been accepted, it would have been because of American pressures, and could thus have fostered an earlier
break between the United States and Western Europe.

Moreover, it was unrealistic to press for a European
Defense Community since France, during most of the
fifties, was not able to play a full role in European
affairs. She had a succession of weak governments and
was deeply involved in bitter, debilitating struggles to
preserve the vestiges of empire, first in Indo-China and
then in Algeria.

With General de Gaulle's re-emergence on the European scene in 1958, the way was open for the liquidation of France's Algerian commitment and for the
restoration of France to a position of strength in
Europe. This restoration caused some concern in
Washington. De Gaulle's conception of a united
Europe stretching from the Atlantic to the Urals,
united not under a supranational political authority
but by the free choice of sovereign governments, challenged the prevailing State Department idea of Euro-

pean unity in a United States of Europe.

Fearful that the Germans would move closer to the French in keeping with the agreement that had been reached between the two governments in 1963, we tried to give Germany a choice of Paris or Washington. Then, to be sure that the Germans would choose Washington, various devices were suggested to create the appearance of shared responsibility for the nuclear defense of Europe or for the finger on the nuclear trigger.

NATO under our urging took up the proposals for mixed-manned vessels and multilateral forces. One ship was even sent on highly publicized voyages to demonstrate the "feasibility" of the concept of mixed-manning.

Europe refused the multilateral nuclear force proposal. If it had not, Western Europe would have been sharply divided between those who found the MLF plan acceptable and those, particularly the British and the French, who did not. The MLF, far from providing a more credible deterrent, would not have changed the responsibility of the United States for the nuclear protection of Europe and probably would have forced the Soviet Union to develop some form of belligerent countermeasure.

When President de Gaulle announced his intention to withdraw from NATO's integrated military structure, the initial response of the State Department did not indicate that U.S. government officials had given much thought or attention to the problem of our future relations with Europe or with France or with de Gaulle.

As André Fontaine has written of de Gaulle:

The arrogance of the President of the Republic is disagreeable and even incomprehensible to his allies; but it is not the arrogance of an isolated

man, otherwise it would be only ridiculous. It is
the arrogance of a man who is not resigned to anything which writes *finis* to a nation about which
history has spoken without a break for a thousand
years.*

In the days following de Gaulle's NATO announce-
ment, four formal meetings and much informal persua-
sion were required to obtain the agreement of the
thirteen other NATO participants to a common response to France. The language of that response suggested not only the caution of the Europeans in
reluctantly agreeing to the American attempt to isolate
France, but also showed our reliance on concepts
which the developments of the past fifteen years had
made irrelevant. Most disturbing were the suggestions
that we would try to continue the policy of the fifties
without France—form without substance—and that
the United States might be ready to abandon efforts
for a united Europe rather than accept change in the
elaborate structure of "military integration." NATO
would simply pack up and move to Belgium; plans
would be made "around" France. "The NATO crisis
is over," Undersecretary of State George Ball, a leader
of the movement to isolate de Gaulle or force him to
remain in NATO, told the Foreign Relations Committee. It was "over," he said, because the fourteen
were determined to continue to press forward with
full vigor to maintain the integrated military structure
without France.

The fact is that there was little agreement within
the alliance as to what NATO should do in the future
or even as to what its purposes should be. Nor was
attention given to some relevant facts. First, over the
years the original NATO had been turned into a
military instrument; second, NATO had become, in its

* André Fontaine, "What is French Policy?" *Foreign Affairs,*
October 1966.

most important manifestation, a military bureaucracy concerned with managerial and technical problems, worried about its own growth and the development of its infrastructure, and with the carrying out of war-game exercises based on prospective Soviet military thrusts in Europe; third, the real deterrent to the threat of Soviet aggression was the American nuclear arsenal; and fourth, despite the structure which NATO developed, the American troops stationed in Europe were essentially hostages to guarantee the American commitment to Europe's defense.

Years of United States predominance in Europe have made it difficult for us to accept a lesser role, but United States policy is beginning to move in a direction which, if ambiguous, at least offers hope that policy makers may come to terms with the realities of the situation across the Atlantic.

On October 7, 1966, in a speech before the National Conference of Editorial Writers meeting in New York City, President Johnson outlined the American approach to Europe:

> We must turn to one of the great unfinished tasks of our generation: making Europe whole. Our purpose is not to overturn other governments, but to help the people of Europe achieve:
> —a continent in which the peoples of Eastern and Western Europe work together for the common good;
> —a continent in which alliances do not confront each other in bitter hostility, but provide a framework in which West and East can act together to assure the security of all. . . .

Stability in Europe can be built only on the basis of a cooperation, or at least an accommodation, that includes England, France, and Germany. Overemphasis on American cooperation with any one power, or an effort to isolate any one of them, is dangerous.

A NATO clearly dominated by the United States is no longer acceptable to our allies. Canadian Prime Minister L. B. Pearson, in a speech at the Atlantic Union Award dinner in Springfield, Illinois on June 11, 1966, stated the case in these words:

> France, and not only France, feels that continental Europe is now strong enough . . . to be given its rightful share in the control of the policies of the Alliance.

We must be willing to build our policy from strength, from the bonds of unity that do exist. We must not destroy these bonds by precipitous or punitive policies nor by insistence upon structures and policies which insure, or are thought to insure, domination by the United States and subordination of others.

We must build on the past fifteen years of fruitful cooperation with European nations in nonmilitary areas, particularly those of trade and monetary policy, and we must make a far more serious effort to develop the purpose set forth in Article 2 of the North Atlantic Treaty: "The Parties . . . will seek to eliminate conflict in their international economic policies and will encourage economic collaboration between any or all of them."

We must adjust to the change of Soviet strategy in Europe and seek to reduce tensions further. In this respect, the effort of President Johnson to begin "peaceful engagement" with the East is a significant step in the right direction.

While maintaining a deterrent against Soviet aggression, we must seek to reduce tensions, even though a general European settlement may be far off. As we look to the 1970's, we must certainly consider possibilities that were out of the question in the 1950's.

A major objective, which at all times is of overriding importance, is progress toward an effective nuclear control agreement. Such an agreement must recognize that France is now a nuclear power and that the French and other Europeans have an interest in their *own* defense. It must also take into account the fear that remains in the minds of many Europeans of a German nuclear capability.

The formation in Germany of the Grand Coalition with the Social Democrats in late 1966 may indicate that Germany is beginning to move away from the course which she had followed under the influence of Konrad Adenauer. The British press called German government reorganization the end of the Bonn-Washington axis—certainly an overstatement. However, if there is some change in German policy, the United States must not be moved immediately to try to punish Bonn, as we previously tried to punish Paris for insufficient solidarity with the NATO ideal.

We must, therefore, recognize that reducing tensions in Europe may eventually open the way to a nonaggression pact between the NATO countries and the Warsaw Pact nations. Only on such terms and in such a context can we look forward to building a Europe of independent strength and influence.

7

Africa and
the Middle East:
Patience Pays

Only in recent years have we begun to realize that all of Africa is not divided into three parts. We have tended to regard North Africa as quite apart from the rest of the continent, despite the fact that throughout much of history the Sahara has served as a bridge, as well as a barrier, and was crisscrossed by trade routes over which caravans carried salt, gold, and other products between the north and the cities and villages of West Africa on the Niger River and the Gulf of Guinea.

Because of its Moslem religious bonds, Islam never regarded the western Sudan area, including Chad, Niger, Mali, Mauritania, and northern Nigeria, as cut off from the Middle East, and the United Arab Republic has tried to exert influence in the area.

South Africa is not a white enclave, and the central African peoples, because of a diversity of influences on Africa, although they may be Negro, are of different ethnic stocks and different language groups. The Ethiopians and the Somalis are ethnically different from the peoples of West Africa and the Bantu groups of central and southern Africa.

The African peoples were subject, as well, to different experiences of European colonial rule. The British tended to emphasize indirect rule, particularly in Uganda and Nigeria, by using existing institutions. The French sought to develop Frenchmen; all Africans were to be made a part of the French culture and tradition, and the French system of education, designed to produce an elite society, was established.

The most consistent colonial exploitation was in the former Belgian Congo. For years the Congo was held as a personal fief by King Leopold of Belgium, who refused to account for it, even to his own government.

Portuguese rule in Africa has also been repressive. Although the Portuguese have never had the kind of color bar that was characteristic of some colonies, very few Africans ever appear to achieve the status of *assimilado*. Absence of color prejudice cannot alone compensate for the lack of education, inadequate economic opportunity, and forced labor which characterize Portugal's "overseas provinces."

Many of Africa's problems today are legacies of colonialism. The political boundaries, to a large extent, make little sense from the African social or economic point of view. They were often drawn by the European powers for reasons of commerce or of European politics during the nineteenth century. In many areas, they cut across tribal lines, separating peoples and creating problems of national identity and national unity. In other areas, artificial unity, created for purposes of administration by the former colonial power, has caused problems. One of the most serious of these is in Nigeria, Africa's most populous country and frequently cited in past years as a showcase for the West. Serious divisions exist in culture, in attitude toward modernization, and in religion between the traditional Moslem north and the more modern, faster developing non-Moslem south. The south, too, has its own problems of division.*

Across the continent, on the shores of the Indian Ocean, the Somali people occupy not only the area of

* Since this chapter was written, the declaration of independence by the eastern region indicated a possible breakup of Nigeria.

the Somali Republic, but also French Somaliland and areas of Ethiopia and Kenya, at least on a nomadic basis.

Problems of national unity plague Uganda, a federation of kingdoms of which Buganda is the largest, with strong separatist tendencies. And instability continues to characterize the Congo and many other areas of Africa.

A second major legacy of colonialism was Western-style government. Because the African states wanted independence quickly, they accepted, in most cases, the style of government they were offered by the mother country, or, with independence, they set up the kind of Western-style government with which they were familiar.

A third legacy of colonialism is a psychological one which derives from the experience of slavery and economic exploitation. Chartered companies rather than governments themselves took charge of economic exploitation of the colonies in many cases, and this tradition influences ideas of economic development today.

The major political problems of Africa today are problems between states, which are in many cases the result of the boundary patterns drawn during the colonial era, and problems of minority governments within states.

Problems between states include the irredentist issues, such as Morocco's claiming both Mauritania and large parts of the Algerian Sahara, and Somalia's seeking to unite those Somalis who live beyond the frontiers of the Somali Republic.

Many interstate problems are the result of tribal migrations. The Bakongo people, for example, live on both sides of the frontier between Angola and the Congo. In the eastern Congo, migrations from Rwanda and Burundi occur as a result of the social problems between tribal groups. Difficulties also result from economic migrations in West Africa and the movement of workers from Upper Volta into Ghana and the Ivory Coast.

Much more severe are the political and racial problems in the countries ruled by minority governments: the Portuguese territories of Angola and Mozambique, Rhodesia, and the Republic of South Africa. We can anticipate that frustration of African desires for elementary political and social justice will lead to increasing tensions in years to come.

What should our African policy be?

The United States has traditionally played a minor role in Africa. In the past, we tended to regard the continent of Africa largely as the responsibility of Britain and France, of the United Nations, and, since their achievement of independence, of the African states themselves.

We did not share in the imperialist adventures of the nineteenth century by which Africa was carved up into colonies and areas of influence by the European powers. After World War I, we supported the establishment of international responsibility, under the League of Nations, for the former Germany colonies.

Our exploitation of Africa was in the earlier period, during the bitter years when Africans by the millions were herded to the coast and transported as slaves to the plantations of the Americas.

On the whole, after World War II, we favored the liquidation of empires and the establishment of independent African nations. To some extent, our concern for freedom and self-determination was held in check by our desire not to embarrass or put too much pressure on the colonial powers who were our NATO allies, but, in general, American support for independence was consistent.

When the most serious crisis in independent Africa occurred in the former Belgian Congo in 1960, we rejected the plea for American intervention and supported the move to turn the Congo problem over to the United Nations.

Many difficulties attended the United Nations effort in the Congo, and its performance has been much criticized. Yet, considering that this was the first effort at peacekeeping on such a scale by the United Nations, and also that the organization was largely unprepared for a test of such magnitude, it did very well.

Our African policy should continue to be one of restraint and of patience. We should respect, encourage, support, and strengthen the efforts of the United Nations and its agencies in dealing with African problems.

We should offer and provide economic and technological aid on a nonpolitical basis, through international organizations or directly, so far as we can, and avoid the soup-kitchen approach of demanding political concessions as the price of minimal aid.

We should be more hesitant about becoming involved in arms build-ups, especially in North Africa where a pattern of countries armed alternately by Russia and by the United States is emerging.

Even though we may discount some of the analysis of Henry Steele Commager, we should proceed with some modesty and humility in the face of the possibility that we are witnessing, and not just witnessing, but are involved in what he describes as:

> . . . the greatest revolution since the discovery of America and the transfer of the center of historical gravity from the Mediterranean to the Atlantic. That is the revolt of Asia and Africa against the West, and the emergence into modernity of

perhaps two-thirds of the peoples of the globe. What we are witnessing seems like the breakup of the great firmament itself; the upheaval of peoples and civilizations, the throwing off of centuries of misrule and exploitation, the convulsive efforts to catch up in a single generation with the progress which the West made, painfully and with almost limitless bloodshed and war and revolution, over a period of four of five centuries.*

Middle East Problems

The problems of the Middle East resemble those of Africa for in both areas underdeveloped nations are seeking to confront the forces of nationalism and the rising expectations of peoples. In the Middle East, more concentrated oil reserves and the existence of Israel present additional complications. Instability has been the mark of the Middle East throughout this century and is likely to be its mark for many years to come.

There is little to be gained by equivocation with reference to Israel and our commitment of support. The legal case for our involvement in the Middle East is one that we can clearly trace back to 1945 when President Truman first asked the British to admit Jewish refugees into Palestine. Our involvement was strengthened in 1947 when we supported the United Nations General Assembly in its call for the partition of Palestine and for the establishment of a Jewish state and an Arab state.

When the State of Israel was proclaimed in 1948, we supported it with immediate recognition. We did not

* *Changing American Attitudes Toward Foreign Policy,* Hearing before the Committee on Foreign Relations, U.S. Senate, 90th Cong., 1st sess., 1967, p. 10.

stop short with general endorsement and support in the family of nations, but agreed in 1950 to the Tripartite Declaration with the objectives of heading off an arms race and forestalling aggression in the area. Our agreement in that declaration to support the territorial integrity of all the states of the Middle East was a commitment to the continued existence and integrity of Israel.

Down through the years, each time that that integrity has been challenged, each time we have been called upon to make public a position, our government speaking through the President has reiterated that commitment.

President Eisenhower reiterated it when in 1957 he spoke of freedom of the seas and the right of Israel to have access to all the oceans of the world. In 1963 President Kennedy reaffirmed our support of Israel and of its integrity. And in May of 1967, President Johnson renewed and reiterated all of these earlier commitments by the United States.

Our commitment to Israel is not limitted to that contained in cold and formal documents and papers. It is also a moral commitment arising from several considerations. Support for the establishment of Israel was not just a formal act but one which reflected the deep sense of responsibility on the part of this nation. In part, in supporting Israel we were rejecting responsibility and not facing up to the realistic need for a more liberal American immigration policy at the end of World War II, but our support also reflected a continuing commitment that is as old as the United States. This commitment was restated in the discouraging context of World War II by Franklin Roosevelt in his Four Freedoms speech when he set forth as the goals for all people: freedom of speech, freedom of worship, freedom from want, and freedom from fear.

Despite clear legal and moral obligations, our policies preceding the Middle East war of June 1967 were not clear or consistent. After our involvement in the Suez crisis of 1956, we should have insisted that the Suez Canal be open to all nations. We should have pressed more vigorously for a clear definition of "innocent passage" with reference to the Gulf of Aqaba and, as a leading maritime nation, we should have assumed responsibility for free use by all nations of that waterway. We not only failed to prevent the buildup of arms among the nations of the Middle East, but actually became one of the principal suppliers. We have been less than fully responsive in seeking an equitable solution to the Arab refugee problem.

The Israeli victory in the brief war of June 1967 brought about a significant alteration in the power relationships in the Middle East and created an opportunity for achieving a greater measure of stability in that area of the world.

Our commitment to Israel today is, if anything, more important and significant than it was before. In fulfilling this commitment, we should: first, again work to assure that the right to life and existence of Israel is recognized by all nations.

Second, we should affirm unequivocally the international character of the waters of the Gulf of Aqaba and the Strait of Tiran, and we should assert, support, and assure the right of all nations to use of the Suez Canal.

Third, we should use our influence to bring about a moratorium or limitation on the influx of arms into the Middle East.

Fourth, we should work with new vigor for a solution to the Arab refugee problem.

Fifth, we should support, with other nations if possible, the border adjustments necessary to assure to Israel the security to which that nation has the right and also to give assurance and stability to those Arab nations that have shown an interest in peace and order. We should be prepared to guarantee these borders, preferably by treaty with other powers and with the support of the United Nations.

8

Micronesia:
Our Trust

Recent trips by President Johnson to Honolulu, Guam, and Asia have given renewed emphasis to the presence of the United States as a Pacific power.

Across the broad expanse of the Pacific and around its periphery, American garrisons and American bases have been built, and are being expanded and strengthened at a rate unprecedented in our history. We are pouring enormous sums of money into the construction of two important bases on the Asian mainland, at Cam Ranh Bay in South Vietnam and at Sattahip in Thailand, supplementing our existing bases in Korea, in the Philippines, in Japan, on Guam, and on Okinawa. We maintain large numbers of troops on the fringes of the Asian mainland.

But there are also in this vast expanse of the Pacific scattered islands known officially as the United States Trust Territory of the Pacific Islands or, more commonly, as Micronesia.

Micronesia comprises some two thousand islands, with a total land area of some seven hundred square miles. On the ninety-seven islands that are regularly inhabited there are approximately ninety thousand people.

Three groups of islands make up the trust territory: the Marianas, the Carolines, and the Marshalls. They were taken from Japan during the Second World War, and are administered by the United States under a trusteeship agreement between the United States and the Security Council of the United Nations. These islands do not fall into the category of U. S. territories like Guam, which, though geographically a part of Micronesia, has been a possession of the United States since the end of the last century. The Pacific islands are not U. S. possessions; they are wards of the international community, with the United States acting as a kind of foster parent to whose care they have been entrusted.

When the trusteeship agreement with the United Nations was concluded, the United States insisted the area be designated a "security trust," the only one of its kind. This gives us the right to fortify the islands, to station troops there, and to close them to outsiders in the interest of U.S. national security. As Secretary of State George Marshall noted, in testifying in favor of the trusteeship agreement before the Committee on Foreign Relations in 1947, although "we must observe certain forms, we have . . . almost complete liberty of action" in the area.

There is some question whether even the forms have been observed in the twenty years during which the United States has exercised jurisdiction over these islands, and we cannot take particular pride in our stewardship. We have not spent very much on such things as schools, roads, sanitary facilities, or even housing. In 1954, to carry out our obligations to promote the political, economic, social, and educational advancement of the people of Micronesia in accordance with our agreement with the United Nations, the Congress appropriated only $7.5 million. The annual appropriation was increased to $17.5 million in 1962, in the wake of a report by a United Nations mission which visited the territory to determine the extent to which the United States was fulfilling its obligations.

A later United Nations mission, which visited the area in 1964, while noting that some progress had been made and while recognizing the formidable problems that distance and inadequacy of transportation present, still felt obliged to note that the United States had come nowhere near fulfilling its stated objectives for the area.

Early in 1966, a team from the World Health Organization visited Micronesia. It found there is still a high incidence of such diseases as leprosy, amoebic dysentery, and tuberculosis, all of which are almost unknown or are completely controlled in the United States and which could be controlled in the trust territory. Gastroenteritis due to poor sanitation is common throughout the territory and is a major cause of child mortality; and there is not one Micronesian doctor who has reached the M.D. level.

The World Health Organization team also found a shortage of other medical personnel and facilities. Much equipment required replacement, and the maintenance of existing facilities and equipment was termed inadequate. A well-defined program for leprosy control was found wanting, and tuberculosis control needed to be revived and pursued systematically. Environmental sanitation was found to be "in the initial stages of development." All this after twenty years of United States administration!

Roads in the trust territory are inadequate; yet essential programs of education, health, and economic development clearly depend on an adequate road system.

Although progress is being made in education, with English the language of instruction, education has suffered from the bureaucratic impasse that arises with respect to the trust territory. Agencies of the U.S. government responsible for programs within the United States feel they cannot operate in Micronesia because it is not "domestic"; yet we cannot give foreign aid to Micronesia because it is not "foreign."

For several years, a similar impasse held up what promises to be one of our more important efforts, the sending of Peace Corps volunteers to Micronesia. The Peace Corps finally decided it could operate in Micronesia because the territory is not a U. S. possession, and in 1967 the Peace Corps had 485 volunteers serving in a program which the agency director termed "an all-out attack on disease, on illiteracy, on methods of increasing productivity, and diversifying production." But during Senate consideration of the 1967 Peace Corps authorization bill, questions were raised in the Foreign Relations Committee and in the Senate itself about the high concentration of Peace Corps volunteers in Micronesia, there being one volunteer for every 195 Micronesians in 1967. The Foreign Relations Committee felt that the aims of the Peace Corps program in Micronesia were "admirable." In its report to the Senate on the bill, however, it questioned "whether they are consistent with the mandate Congress gave the Peace Corps."

The committee report continued, "It may even be questioned whether the Peace Corps ought to be in Micronesia at all. It is a U. S. trust territory and if the United States has fulfilled its trust to the inhabitants badly then those responsible for this condition ought to be also responsible for its remedy." This consideration and considerations of economy in light of the expenses connected with the Vietnam War led to a reduction in the Senate in the 1967 Peace Corps authorization request.

Progress in education raises several questions that are fundamental to the future of the territory and to the role of the United States in that future.

The theory that we should just let the Micronesians be happy in their simple life and ignorance is untenable. Micronesia is in the modern world, and we cannot remove it. We cannot return the Pacific islands to the era of the "simple savage," the ideal of eighteenth-century Europe before what Alan Moorehead calls "the fatal impact" of Western civilization.

We fail as a government, and particularly as a liberal democracy, if we fail to provide the essential service of government to a people who, through the mischance of history rather than through their own choice, have become dependent on the United States.

Our responsibility to the international community as far as the Trust Territory of the Pacific Islands is concerned includes political advancement toward self-government or independence. The United States has been subject to increasing criticism at the United Nations not only for its neglect of the economic and social needs of the territory but for the slowness of its political development.

What of the future of Micronesia? Three possibilities appear to exist. First, the territory may eventually achieve independence, a hope frequently expressed in the United Nations. For several reasons, however, independence does not appear to be a particularly desirable course, even to most Micronesians. As far as the United States is concerned, the security considerations which at the end of the Second World War dictated the maintenance of control over the islands are somewhat altered with the development of long-range missiles and the establishment of U.S. bases on the Asian mainland, but the necessity to deny control of the area to any other power must still weigh heavily in the minds of Pentagon strategists. As far as the Micronesians themselves are concerned, not even the United Nations mission could find any significant sentiment in the islands for independence, particularly if independence would mean loss of the American subsidy. The population of less than one hundred thousand and the limited economic potential argue against independence.

Second, it has been suggested that ultimately Micronesia might be affiliated with Guam or become a part of the state of Hawaii. Aspects of these proposals remain to be explored, but there are several evident disadvantages, notably the distances involved and the different levels of development in Hawaii and on Guam.

Third, some form of continuing association with the United States might be worked out. A status comparable to that of Puerto Rico for example, might eventually be found suitable for Micronesia.

The United States has been challenged repeatedly in the United Nations, particularly by the Soviet Union, to subject the future of the islands to a plebiscite.

The United Nations mission concluded that a plebiscite now would result in an overwhelming expression of sentiment in favor of affiliation with the United States. But a plebiscite today would not offer the islanders a real choice. We would be saying, in effect, you can go off on your own in the great wide world without us, or you can continue to put up with us and with our assistance.

In defending its exercise of its responsibility in the trust territory before the United Nations, the United States was able to escape severe criticism only because our delegation was able to report that a greatly expanded program was being proposed to the U. S. Congress. In May of 1966, the Congress was asked to authorize $172 million for a five-year capital development program for the trust territory, but the program was not enacted. In 1967, however, the annual appropriation was raised.

If the U. S. Congress is not prepared to spend the money urgently required to meet our responsibilities to the Micronesians and thus to the international community to which we are responsible for their welfare, then certain steps must be taken lest the United States stand justly accused of the kinds of policies for which we have faulted the European colonial powers.

First, the Trust Territory of the Pacific Islands should be accorded the same treatment with respect to our tariffs as those territories which are U. S. possessions. The Customs Simplification Act of 1954, which was calculated to stimulate the development of light industry in U.S. possessions, provides that the growth and products of a U. S. insular possession outside the customs area of the United States are free of duty when imported into the U. S. customs area if they do not contain foreign materials to the value of more than 50 percent of their total value. A similar provision for the trust territory would be an incentive to economic development, particularly if combined with a free flow of capital.

Second, the islands should be opened to tourists. The area has been treated as a kind of private property by the Defense Department, which restricted travel on alleged grounds of security. But, with the exception of the missile test site at Kwajalein, there are no major U. S. installations in the area. (Guam is not considered to be in the area.) Distance perhaps precludes Micronesia's ever becoming an American tourist playground comparable to the Virgin Islands, but Americans are not the only tourists. Micronesia was once known as the Japanese Riviera, and tourism is a potential source of income.

Third, if the U.S. Congress is not going to provide sufficient funds for capital improvement, then we should not seal off this area as an exclusively American economic preserve. It is only within the last few years that American private capital has been permitted into the area. We should permit other nations to move in and help develop Micronesia, improving potentially important industries, such as fishing.

The era of mercantilism and colonialism is past. When a nation assumes rights over another nation or people, it also assumes obligations. We require, or believe we require, these rights in Micronesia and we cannot evade the responsibilities and obligations. It is time that they be met.

9

Vietnam:
In Dubious Battle

Vietnam is a very special problem, outside of the context of general Asian problems and outside of the context of world problems largely because of the quantitative measure of our commitment to what was until recently considered a minor if not residual responsibility and concern.

Quite suddenly and surprisingly we have found ourselves involved in the third largest war in our history and involved under terms and conditions which are different from any we have known in the past.

Vietnam is a military problem. Vietnam is a political problem; and as the war goes on it has become more clearly a moral problem.

For the first time in our history, at least in this century, we have had to raise questions about the justification for our involvement in a war.

The resolution of the question of the justice or the injustice of a war depends upon three general considerations: (1) purposes and objectives, (2) methods and means, and (3) proportion. Even if we accept that the purpose is good and that the methods are acceptable, one must still raise the practical question of whether or not the evil and the destruction required to win the war are proportionate to the good that may be achieved.

Our involvement in Vietnam must be examined in the light of each of these three considerations.

Our participation in World War I was certainly morally defensible, and in World War II even more clearly so. In each of these wars, also, a reasonably good case could be made for the methods and the instruments we used.

We opposed submarine warfare and poison gas in World War I. By the time World War II had come, submarines were highly respectable.

In World War II, we denounced civilian bombing when it was first initiated and expressed reservations about the use of fire bombs. But as the war went on we began strategic bombing and permitted destruction of Dresden with fire bombs. Then at least we had the defense that we were not the first to use these questionable instruments or methods. Our use of the atomic bomb, however, was of a somewhat different order and raised many questions not yet answered.

We have been fortunate in that the two great modern wars of this century were fought with the weapons of the previous war. There was time to adjust moral judgments. The danger is that the next war may be fought with contemporary weapons.

World War I and World War II were justifiable also by the rule of proportion, since the good which we could anticipate from victory outweighed the harm and the cost of achieving that victory.

What are our objectives in Vietnam? Nearly every possible purpose has been offered, at one time or another, as justification for our involvement.

It is necessary, some say, for the defense of the United States. An extreme presentation of this position was that of a recent candidate for the Senate who said that if we did not fight in the elephant grass of Vietnam, we would have to fight in the rye grass of our western states. Yet, in the early phase of this war, no one ever accepted that our defense perimeter extended as far as Vietnam.

It is necessary, others say, that we take a stand in Vietnam in order to contain China. But few if any of the China-containment men of a few years ago held that the containment of China in any way required us to commit nearly half a million combat troops in Vietnam.

It is argued that we have a legal obligation under the SEATO treaty and other commitments. But the SEATO treaty itself has not been brought into operation in the Vietnam War. South Vietnam has never requested action under SEATO, and any joint action, as provided for in that treaty, would be impossible because of the positions of France and Pakistan, and possibly Britain. The argument of legal obligation is one which the Administration sought to bolster by securing the passage of the Tonkin Gulf Resolution by the Congress in 1964, although the Secretary of State, in testimony before the Foreign Relations Committee, said that even without the Tonkin Gulf Resolution, commitment in Vietnam was defensible and did not depend on the resolution for its legal basis.

It is said that we fight to ensure the credibility of our commitments, to show the world that we honor our treaty obligations. This is the rationale of our politico-military prestige. Yet we have already demonstrated our reliability in Korea and in the protection of Taiwan as well as in Europe.

It is said that we must carry on the war in Vietnam in order to preserve and defend our national honor. Our national honor is not at stake, and should not so readily be offered. In every other great war of the century, we have had the support of what is generally accepted as the decent opinion of mankind. We do not have that today. We cannot, of course, depend only on this opinion to prove our honor; it may not be sound. But always in the past we have not only had this support, but we have used it as a kind of justification for our action.

What about the methods which we are using?

This is a most difficult area for judgment. We are tempted to take the view presented by Cromwell in his reply to Wharton's protest at Pride's Purge and the execution of the King: "It is easy to object to the glorious actings of God if we look too much upon the instruments. Be not offended at the manner. Perhaps there was no other way left."

Civilian bombing and the use of napalm in this theater of war are more difficult to defend than they were when we bombed civilians in retaliation or as incidental to our seeking out military targets in World War II, and used napalm as a sophisticated weapon against an enemy also using sophisticated weapons.

Even the discussion of the war in Vietnam calls for a new vocabulary. George Orwell, writing in 1946 about another war and another nation, in his essay *Politics and the English Language,* described the problem this way:

> Inflated style is itself a kind of euphemism. A mass of Latin words falls upon the facts like soft snow, blurring the outlines and covering up all the details. . . .
>
> Political speech and writing are largely the defence of the indefencible. . . . Defenceless villages are bombarded from the air, the inhabitants driven out into the countryside, the cattle machine-gunned, the huts set on fire with incendiary bullets: this is called *pacification.* Millions of peasants are robbed of their farms and sent trudging along the roads with no more than they can carry: this is called *transfer of population* or *rectification of frontiers.*

The razing of villages and herding of their inhabitants into camps was called *regroupement* when the French were doing it in Algeria. Today in Vietnam we call it "revolutionary development."

The Latin word of importance in this war is "escalation." It has a self-generating power, building and growing on itself.

George Kennan, testifying before the Foreign Relations Committee in 1966, was asked whether he knew of anyone who, when we first sent advisers into Vietnam, had said that he anticipated that these would be followed by more advisers and eventually by combat personnel; whether he knew of anyone who really expected the war to go this way, or who, expecting it to go this way, was in favor of it. He said he knew of no one. It would be somewhat reassuring if we could find someone who anticipated what did happen and understood what was happening.

A second term of significance in this war is "kill-ratio." Reports of our success are given in this measurement; we do not capture hills or take towns or cross rivers. Our operations are more often "search and destroy" than "clear and hold."

The final measurement that must be applied to this as to any war is that of proportion. Three points must be raised. First, assuming that we understand what we mean by victory, is there a possibility of victory? Second, what would be the cost of that victory? Third, what assurance do we have that a better world or a better society will emerge in Vietnam following that victory?

The answers should be positive on each of these three counts. I do not believe that they are positive.

A broad warning is sounded by Arnold J. Toynbee in his work *Hannibal's Legacy*, a study of the effect of the wars with Carthage on the Roman republic. Toynbee says that the price of Rome's subjugation of the Western Mediterranean was an economic, social, and religious derangement of Roman life. The government, bent on pursuing military adventures on the frontiers, became less and less responsive to domestic problems. Toynbee draws the lesson:

> War posthumously avenges the dead on the survivors, and the vanquished on the victors. The

nemesis of war is intrinsic. It did not need the invention of the atomic weapon to make this apparent. It was illustrated, more than two thousand years before our time, by Hannibal's legacy to Rome.

In view of all these considerations, we should hesitate to waste our strength, economic, military, and moral, in so highly questionable a course as the war in Vietnam. Rather we are called upon to exert every effort to bring about some kind of limitation and ultimately a settlement of the war.

We have, I believe, passed several points at which some such limitation might have been possible. One was at the time of the New Year's bombing pause in 1966. Another was in the early summer of 1966 when it was evident that the significant escalation which had taken place in the preceding six months did not promise success and when there was a possibility of following General Gavin's recommendation of a modified enclave policy.

At the present time I see two possibilities: one, that we permit and encourage the United Nations to assume a much stronger role in the efforts to settle the Vietnamese war; and second, as an alternative, that we try the Gavin policy. Under this enclave policy we would reduce the "search and kill" missions. We would not seek military domination and control of the entire country, but would hold strong points in important areas of Vietnam. At the same time as efforts to achieve pacification within the controlled areas were pushed, negotiations with the National Liberation Front over the uncontrolled areas would be attempted; this would be a preliminary to a settlement with Hanoi.

10

China:

Need We Collide?

No other foreign policy matter is subject to as much uncertainty and misunderstanding and fundamental disagreement in the United States as is our China policy. Perhaps in the long run no policy is more significant to the welfare of the country and the peace of the world in the final third of the twentieth century and beyond that into the twenty-first century.

Our approach to the Far East is a guarded one. The "Mysterious East" and the "Inscrutable Orient" are phrases long built into our language. They reflect the fact that we are less sure of ourselves in dealing with peoples of another culture than with those who share our own culture and the tradition of Western civilization. During the last twenty years, this uncertainty and apprehension have been heightened by the growing force of communism in China.

In 1966 a new era in United States understanding of China began. The hearings on Mainland China, held by the Senate Committee on Foreign Relations in 1966, were followed on television by large numbers of Americans. For the first time since those years in the late 1940's and early 1950's when bitter accusations obstructed every attempt to discuss China, the American public was given an opportunity to hear intelligent, reasoned debate on China and its importance today.

For the first time in over twenty years, Americans faced the problem of China in an atmosphere relatively free from accusations and misunderstanding and reasonably free from the myths of the past. The experts and the professional China watchers were not in agreement in their answers to many questions, but all of the hard questions were asked.

From the inquiry and discussions, some facts have

become clear and some conclusions have been reached which may be accepted as a basis for policy evaluation and determination.

There was general agreement that we ought not to think of China in terms of Western concepts and experience. China is a society and a civilization, not a nation state in the Western sense of the term.

The ancient Chinese empire maintained a continuous identity over the same area for over three thousand years of recorded history. Geographical factors encouraged the evolution of a distinctive closed society. China proper was isolated from the other major civilizations by high mountains in the west, the sea on the east and south, and the desert in the north. Where nature had failed to provide a sufficient boundary, the Chinese sought to protect themselves from the incursions of barbarians by building, about the third century B.C., the 1,500-mile Great Wall.

Isolation and the strength of its own culture were the basis for a sense of superiority which characterized the Chinese. In their eyes, China was the Middle Kingdom of the world, the center of the universal empire, surrounded by concentric circles of vassal and barbarian states. The only relationship she acknowledged with other peoples was one whereby other states paid her tribute. There was no conception of a relationship based on the sovereign equality of states, a principle that has been the foundation of international relations in the West since the sixteenth century.

This Chinese attitude toward the outside world persisted through the centuries. The Emperor Ch'ien Lung, who reigned in the eighteenth century, for example, courteously received ambassadors from King George III of England who had come to negotiate a commercial treaty. The Emperor informed them that it was commendable for the English to wish to partake of the benefits of Chinese civilization but that it would be quite impossible for them, at such great distance, to learn even the rudiments of civilized behavior. As for trade, the Emperor said, his celestial empire obviously possessed all things in abundance and had no need for the products of the barbarians.

A distinctive feature of the civilization of Old China was a concern for social order as the supreme value, the basis for the good life. Individualism was not esteemed. Indeed, it is still represented in the Chinese language as a foreign idea, by ideographic characters that suggest selfishness. The ideal was, and is, sacrifice of the individual for the common good.

Traditional Chinese law did not protect the individual; it was administered in the interest of the community. Man was judged not only for his own acts but, under a system of mutual responsibility, was held accountable for the acts of his family or group. The same system is used today by the Communists as a means of social and political control.

It was also accepted that the rulers of China were the guardians of a kind of universal truth, promulgated by a leader who was a "virtuous (or right-acting) man" and that a man should conduct his relations with his fellow men on the basis of the Confucian classical code. According to this code, men were not equal; each had his place and his duties. His responsibilities and his relationships with superiors as well as with inferiors were prescribed by the Confucian code.

The talented were trained in the "true teaching" and selected, through a series of rigorous examinations, to enter official life. The interest of the bureaucracy was, therefore, the maintenance of the system by reiteration of the "true teaching," a system which also kept the social classes under control.

Ideographic writing also served to make communication of new or foreign ideas difficult. While Japan, Korea, and even Vietnam developed systems of writing related to sounds, China maintained the complicated system of symbols which represented meaning (comparable to the way in which a number has a meaning unrelated to a sound). Foreign ideas and concepts thus could not be expressed except in terms of a symbol, a symbol which already had its own significance in the Chinese context.

Rigid though it was, the traditional pre-Communist Chinese system allowed for revolution at the same time. When failure or disintegration of the dynasty's rule made it clear that Heaven had withdrawn its Mandate, a new dynasty might arise and install itself and then claim the support of the people without any question of "legitimacy" through family succession or class ties, as was the case in the West.

No distinction was made in Old China between the person of the ruler and his policies; an attack on one was an attack on the other. Thus, dissent, the concept of the loyal opposition which plays such an important role in Western political thought, was inconceivable.

There are in these traditions some obvious points of identity and of correspondence with Communist ideology and techniques. The Chinese emphasis on community and society, as opposed to individualism and personalism, and the Communist emphasis upon community are not far apart. The Chinese rulers as guardians of the truth, based on the Chinese classics, are functionally not very different from Communist leaders, interpreting the doctrine according to Lenin or Stalin.

On the other hand, there are points of difference and divergence. The traditional closed and self-contained Chinese attitude does not conform to the conception of world-wide communism.

By the middle of the nineteenth century, internal and external pressures on the old Chinese system had built up to an intolerable level. The rapidly expanding population was too much for any administration. In addition, China was challenged by the expanding power and influence of the West, whose military superiority forced the Imperial Government to grant privileges and concessions to foreigners. There was great need for change, but China had no idea of progress or of economic growth; rather, her ideal was conservation of the old ways and reverence for the wisdom of age. Long immersed in herself, convinced of her own superiority, China was not prepared to take foreign ideas into account. Unable to modernize and thus meet the challenges of Western imperialism, she was forced into submission.

As a response to the disintegration of the old system and, in part, as a reaction against humiliation by the Western powers, a wave of nationalism built up over the last half of the nineteenth century.

Chinese nationalism gained its first victory in sweeping aside the imperial dynasty and establishing a republic in 1911, but the hopes of the republican leaders for a democratic society were frustrated and China collapsed into a system of war lords. Disunity and weakness encouraged the renewal of foreign pressure, this time by Japan.

The Chinese republican leader, Dr. Sun Yat-sen, seeking a device to replace the lost cohesion, turned to the idea of party dictatorship, and the Chinese revolution began to look for its inspiration not to the French Revolution, but to the Russian. However, the Nationalist Party (the Kuomintang), organized on the Leninist party model, was never able to establish its control over all of China. In 1950, after some forty years of chaos following the fall of the Manchus, civil wars, and foreign invasions, China attempted unification, this time under the new sociopolitical "religion," Chinese communism.

How is the new revolution going? What we know today is not clear.

By any one of several modes of measurement—

budget figures, numbers of personnel, kinds of programs instituted, activity of the leadership—it seems clear that the main issues on the minds of the top leadership are industrialization, extension of political control within China, transformation of the social climate of the country, and improvement of agriculture.

Publicly, the Chinese leaders state their belief in the forces of anti-imperialism, in the inevitability of the revolution, and in the expansion of the socialist camp beyond national boundaries. Yet the primary task they set themselves in their 1956 constitution is the "socialist transformation" of the society and the economy and the industrialization of their own country.

Even a brief look at modern China impresses one with the truly awesome character of the internal problems she faces. China's good earth has supported more people than that of any other country on this planet. Yet today, the food-population problem is her most serious challenge.

China is estimated to have at present between 750 and 895 million people. The land mass is diverse, but only 11 to 12 percent can be cultivated easily. Some areas may hold yet undeveloped riches, but in terms of physical resources, in comparison with the United States or the Soviet Union, China must be counted a poor country.

For thousands of years "before Liberation," the Communist take-over, farmers tilled the soil using traditional methods, with only slight modern improvements. When the Communists came to power, most of the land that could be cultivated easily was already in use and the potential of traditional methods for raising agricultural yields was almost exhausted.

In the early years, the Communists emphasized industrial development, and expansion was confined largely to the urban and commercial areas. Agriculture was neglected. In recent years, greater emphasis has been placed on agricultural development, but experience during the past decade has demonstrated that there is no easy road to increased agricultural productivity.

In 1958 the ill-fated Great Leap Forward, an attempt to do the impossible in economic development by a program of political and ideological mobilization, was inaugurated. It was a serious miscalculation of what the economy could bear and led to a severe economic crisis, a kind of Communist Great Depression. By 1959 a combination of rising population, limited growth potential of the traditional agricultural technology, and uneven harvests had brought China to the brink of economic collapse. There was widespread malnutrition, although actual famine was averted.

As a result of the disasters of the Great Leap Forward, many of the more ambitious economic goals had to be abandoned and economic policy redefined on a more realistic, pragmatic basis. Agricultural development was re-emphasized, and since 1962 there has been slow recovery in the agricultural sector, so that by 1966 production was at about the level prevailing at the beginning of the Great Leap Forward. The experiment of the Great Leap Forward appears to have cost the Chinese economy roughly a decade of growth.

If China continues her present programs, there is some reason to believe that yields can be raised at a sufficient pace to keep up with expanding population. Yet it appears likely that for some time in the future, agriculture will be unable to supply a net flow of capital to support industrialization. Rather, agriculture will itself require a new flow of resources from the industrial sector, at least part of the time, if food supplies are to be kept up to subsistence level.

Her current trade pattern suggests that China is being forced to spend an increasing proportion of her foreign exchange on food imports, even though she is still short of the technological capacity to produce desperately needed investment goods. Mainland China's wheat imports over the past decade, largely from Canada and Australia, have increased sharply from an average of twenty thousand tons per year in the 1954–1960 period to between five and six million tons per year since 1961. These imports have increased grain supply by 3 to 4 percent, and are expected to continue for the next two to three years.

One study of China's potential progress, which assumed an average economic growth of 5½ to 7½ percent per year over the next twenty years and a population growth rate of about 2 percent, concluded that by 1985 China will have reached approximately the level of per capita income attained in the Soviet Union in the 1930's. Yet, over the same period, the developed world's level will have increased, and thus the real gap between the economic level of the developed world and that of China may well have widened.

Even with increased productivity, however, China is far from solving her basic problem. The absence of war, improved medical practices, and better sanitation have contributed to population growth. China's population is increasing by some 15 million per year, a growth rate of about 2 percent, three times the pre-World War II rate. Feeding the increased population alone will require heroic efforts.

Most observers are convinced that in the absence of large-scale foreign aid (which seems unlikely from any source at present) or a series of unusually good harvests, economic growth and advancement will be slower in coming years. There is always the danger that the impatient leadership will turn again to drastic measures in another desperate attempt to break out of the food-population spiral, and this might lead to an economic crisis of the dimensions of 1959–1961. Even the most optimistic estimates conclude that China's internal problems, solely on the agricultural front, are such that they will continue to absorb, as they do now, the major portion of the time and energy of the Chinese leadership.

In addition to the requirements of agriculture, the increased demand on the economy by the military is also potentially, and perhaps actually, a disruptive factor. Some observers believe that a great military demand could easily use up China's additional productive capacity as quickly as it could be developed. This would, in the long run, or perhaps sooner, lead to serious dislocations. The influence of military demand is one of the more difficult factors to plan for the future. While the present leadership is imbued with the martial spirit, with the ideal of struggle carried over from long years of hardship and bitter conflict which preceded the Communist triumph, the younger generation that will soon replace them may well be less militant and, perhaps, when they are in power, less anxious to maintain a burdensome military establishment, particularly at the expense of economic development or industrialization.

On the political level as well, serious difficulties appear to have arisen, difficulties of which the Great Cultural Revolution and the purges of 1966–1967 were clearly a manifestation.

The first of these problems is the prospective change in a substantial portion of the Chinese leadership over the next few years. The average age of the Politburo is nearly seventy. Mao, seventy-three and in failing health, appears determined to spend his final years— in the tradition of imperial leaders throughout history —arranging for his own deification. Whatever else the Red Guard purges may signify, they have been an attempt to strengthen the hold of the cult of Mao and of the Maoist ideology by rooting out all foreign, bourgeois, and even ancient Chinese influences. The goal seems to have been to make firm the Maoist viewpoint in anticipation of the eventual take-over by younger elements who have not had the inspiration or the galvanizing experience of the heroic years of struggle or of the Long March. Mao clearly intends to try to head off any kind of reaction against Maoism comparable to that which occurred in the Soviet Union after the death of Stalin. He is attempting to assure that there can never be any "de-Maoization."

Great efforts have been made to strengthen the grip of the ideology with pressure for "voluntary" manual labor and intensified study of Mao's works. In spite of these efforts, however, it seems unlikely that the monolithic character and the stability which characterized the top leadership from the beginnings of Chinese communism until 1966, a unity and strength arising from the shared experience of the Long March and the campaigns against the Japanese and the Nationalists, will persist into the second generation. However conclusive the purges of 1966 and 1967 may appear, history suggests that they may have been only a rehearsal for what is to come after Mao's death. Communist regimes seldom manage the transfer of power successfully. Usually discussions within the leadership group reach a deadlock, and a crisis follows, unlike the pattern in a parliamentary system, with the concept of the loyal opposition, where the deadlock may be broken by resignations from the government.

When as important a dictator as Mao passes from the scene, some change is inevitable. The charisma of Mao, his enormous personal prestige as a revolutionary leader, soldier, writer, and thinker, cannot be willed to a successor. China, too, seems to have a problem of generations in politics.

Significant in this respect are the changes that have occurred in the Chinese Communist Party since it came to power in 1949. In the early years, the hard core of the Party was composed of soldiers and leaders of the rural base areas that supported the Red Army. The younger members, products of the party-building programs of the 1950's, are economic planners, factory managers, and others who were selected for advancement on the basis of their skills in administration and modernization. There has been friction between the orthodox old warriors and the better educated younger members who have been promoted on ability. A feature of the 1966–1967 purges was the attempt to reinstate political orthodoxy as the sole criterion for professional advancement, an interesting parallel with the examination system of Old China. This attempt apparently reflects Mao's fear that the younger generation lacks revolutionary zeal and his suspicion of the more professional and pragmatic orientation of the younger party members. Adolescents, who presumably have not yet had a chance to develop a middle-class outlook, have been used as the lever in the Cultural Revolution, indicating that the older leadership may lack confidence in the party's middle generation. Apparently, they did not trust the Party to do the job.

The conclusion must be that, while China will continue to talk a World Power game, even with nuclear weapons her principal concern and effort must remain domestic and internal.

Yet, China's foreign policy objectives are of great concern to us and there is significant disagreement about her ability to pursue these objectives successfully.

One of the most important, if not *the* most important, foreign policy objective of the Chinese today is to achieve recognition as a Great Power whose voice is heard in the world's councils. China, understandably, seeks to overcome the bitter legacy of a hundred years of humiliation by the West. Recognition as a Great Power is essentially a nationalistic, rather than an ideological, objective. All Chinese, Communist and non-Communist, agree on its importance.

Combined with reassertion of China's historic role as a major power are two corollary objectives: recovery of the "lost territories," and re-establishment of the predominant Chinese influence in Southeast Asia.

The "lost territories" to be recovered include Hong Kong, Macao, parts of Soviet Asia, Tibet, Taiwan and the off-shore islands, and land along the Sino-Indian frontier. This is also an essentially nationalistic objective, shared by all Chinese. In Chinese eyes, it is not an expansionist position, for they consider that these territories were taken forcibly from China by the unequal treaties imposed on her during the nineteenth century or, in the case of Taiwan, were denied to her by the military power of the U.S. Seventh Fleet.

Supporters of an interventionist policy for the United States in Eastern Asia invariably cite the famous essay of Chinese Defense Minister Marshal Lin Piao, published in September 1965, to support the thesis that China is bit by bit embarking on world conquest. We are told that Marshal Lin's essay, *Long Live the Victory of the People's War*, is a blueprint for aggression, just as surely as *Mein Kampf* was a blueprint for Hitler's conquest of Europe. We are assured that our failure to take Lin's words at face value will spur the Chinese on to new adventures.

"Case studies in the anatomy and physiology of aggression" are reported to show how "the spread of domination feeds on itself, kindling fires within the aggressor country and weakening the will of the potential victims." Aggression by Japan in Manchuria in 1931, by Mussolini in Ethiopia in 1935, and by Hitler in Europe in World War II is frequently evoked.

Three examples of Chinese aggression in recent years are usually cited: Korea, Tibet, and the Sino-Indian frontier. These instances, along with sporadic shelling of the off-shore islands of Quemoy and Matsu, are offered in support of the thesis that China has embarked on the conquest of Asia and eventually of the world. Let us examine briefly the cases cited.

Korea: What the United Nations officially labeled Chinese aggression in Korea was, in fact, a move which the Chinese considered, with some justification given the statements of U.S. military leaders at the time, a defense of their vital interests close to their own frontier. It now seems clear that the invasion of South Korea was not Chinese inspired, but a product of Soviet and North Korean planning. The Chinese Communists apparently did not intend to become involved in Korea when the war started; they were much too busy consolidating power at home. (The Communists had come to power in October of 1949, and the invasion took place in June of 1950.) However, when American troops crossed the 38th parallel into North Korea, the Chinese became very apprehensive. Not only did they fear for the survival of the North Korean regime, but the American drive to the Yalu River appeared to threaten China itself, particularly the industrial heartland of Manchuria. Probably there was also grave concern over Soviet influence in North Korea.

There had been warnings from Peking that if United Nations (largely American) forces crossed the 38th parallel, the Chinese would consider it a threat to a vital interest. But, bolstered by assurances from our generals and State Department experts that the Chinese would not come in, we decided to ignore the warnings.

The Sino-Indian Frontier: The case of the Sino-Indian frontier is more complex, and here the Chinese case is not clear. Portions of the border between China and India have been in dispute for many years. Three areas are involved in the conflicting territorial claims. First, in the western sector, the territory of Aksai-Chin in the Ladakh region contains some fifteen thousand square miles of disputed territory. Here the definition of the boundary rest on the Tibet-Ladakh agreement of 1684, the Dogra-Ladakh exchange of

1842, and the two Anglo-Chinese notes of 1846–1847 and 1899.

The second, or central sector, the area of least conflict, contains some two hundred square miles of disputed territory. While no major treaty exists delineating the boundary, the territory has been under Indian administration since the seventeenth century.

The third, or eastern area, is what India calls the North East Frontier Agency (NEFA). It comprises thirty-two thousand square miles. Here the issue is the validity of the McMahon line, which China does not recognize on the grounds that she never ratified the Simla convention of 1914.

The areas are clearly the subject of conflicting claims, claims difficult to adjust or even to define precisely, for the border passes through some of the most inhospitable terrain in the world.

It also appears that the Chinese took the initiative in the incidents of 1962. However, some experts have suggested that there was provocation in the building of Indian posts further and further into the disputed territory, as well as in certain statements by Prime Minister Nehru to the effect that India intended to take back all the claimed territory then held by China.

China was the aggressor on the Indian border, but the context is such that it gives no support to any claim that this incident proves China plans to take over India.

Tibet: The Kingdom of Tibet has a long history of close relations with China. For a number of centuries, the Chinese regarded Tibet as part of the Chinese Empire. The outside world has generally recognized a kind of Chinese suzerainty over Tibet; at least, no one has ever formally recognized Tibet as an independent country. But Tibet does have a separate, non-Chinese culture, and could, by the criteria that are accepted today, claim the right to independence.

The Chinese traditionally ruled Tibet as a kind

of colony, with a loose administration which respected, in general, the Tibetan social and religious institutions. Most scholars do not, therefore, regard Peking's determination to reassert control over Tibet (a control that the Nationalist Chinese claimed from the first but were never able to enforce and a control that had been accepted, willingly or unwillingly in varying degrees, by the Tibetans for a thousand years) as "aggression" in any sense comparable to the Italian conquest of Ethiopia. One can oppose Chinese rule in Tibet and can condemn the social and cultural repression of the Tibetans without concluding that the reestablishment of Chinese rule was necessarily China's first step on the road to world domination.

China shares a 4,500 mile border with the Soviet Union and has claimed parts of Soviet Central Asia and the Soviet Far East, which she maintains were taken from her in the nineteenth century by Czarist Russia. There have been sporadic, but persistent reports of incidents, sometimes involving substantial numbers of troops along the border in Central Asia. Soviet President Nikolai Podgorny has warned that the Soviet people are alert and determined to protect their Far Eastern territories against any invaders.

China has not pressed her territorial claims against the Soviet Union, even during those periods when Sino-Soviet relations were at a very low ebb.

China clearly seeks re-establishment of what she considers to be her traditional sphere of influence in Southeast Asia. Historically, Chinese influence in the area ebbed and flowed with the strength of the central government in China, and the form and nature of the relationship varied from state to state, although Chinese influence penetrated perhaps most heavily into that area we now call Vietnam. Chinese political domination has not been clear or consistent, at least not since the tenth century when Vietnam achieved "independence" from China. At times the relationship appears to have meant little more than tacit agreement not to aid China's enemies.

The argument that China seeks to conquer Southeast Asia in order to have control of the "rice bowl" is not very strong. While Burma, Thailand, Cambodia, and South Vietnam in 1963 accounted for 55 percent of the world's rice exports, those exports totaled only 3.7 million tons. The 1965 grain output of China was about 180 million tons. Thus even if the Chinese wished to assure themselves of the full supply they could presumably obtain through trade without resorting to conquest, the increase in supply would be only marginal. It should also be noted that China, while importing wheat in recent years, has been exporting rice.

A type of benevolent neutrality may well be the minimum condition for Southeast Asia acceptable to China today, but it may also be the outside limit of Chinese ambition.

Given China's desire for recognition as a Great Power as its main foreign policy objective, the second major tenet of Chinese foreign policy on which there is wide agreement is China's determination to eradicate United States military power from the Asian mainland and, as far as possible, United States influence as well. This is tied in with China's desire to be recognized as a Great Power. Although it conforms to Communist ideological opposition to democratic philosophy, it is basically nationalistic and there is little reason to believe that a non-Communist Chinese government would welcome a U. S. military presence on the Asian mainland any more than the present government in Peking does.

China's pretensions to leadership of a world revolution are frequently cited as justification for an activist, interventionist U. S. foreign policy.

But is China in fact leading the Communist World Revolution? Although there is every reason to believe that the leaders in Peking are firmly convinced that their revolution will serve as a model for the developing world and for the eventual defeat of the industrial "cities" by the countryside of the "people," in reality, the Chinese experience has, with one significant exception, almost no relevance outside China. In no other country or part of the world do precisely the same conditions exist under which the Chinese Communists achieved power. Mao was able to gain control of China because he gained leadership of the Chinese nationalist movement, consolidating and leading it against a foreign invader in World War II. Only in Vietnam has this feat been duplicated. Ho Chi Minh is the only Communist leader in the underdeveloped world who was able to gain control of his country's nationalist movement at the time of resistance to a foreign invasion.

(It is frequently asserted that the United States effort in Vietnam is responsible for the failure of the Communists to gain control of Indonesia, but responsible observers are convinced that the anti-Communist events of late 1965 were the result of forces and conflicts within the Indonesian society itself.)

China's attack on India in 1962 and her support of Pakistan on the Kashmir issue have dealt a severe blow to whatever hope Indian Communists might have had for capitalizing on that country's internal problems and divisions.

The ultimatum to India during the brief Indo-Pakistani War represented China not only as a warlike power anxious to take advantage of the struggles within the Third World, but as weak when the ultimatum had to be withdrawn. And Peking's rival, the

Soviet Union, appeared to all the world as the peace-maker at Tashkent.

In Japan, the pro-Chinese Communist Party has followed the Peking line at great cost. Its failure to support the nuclear test ban treaty appears to have isolated the party by alienating the trade unions and the powerful Japanese Socialist Party. Even North Korea has now proclaimed its "neutrality" in the Sino-Soviet struggle.

China's lack of success in Africa has also been noteworthy. In September 1965, President Nasser of the United Arab Republic, returning home after a successful visit to Moscow, announced that the Soviet Union should be invited to the Afro-Asian conference scheduled to meet in Algiers, an invitation Peking had been most anxious to thwart. (The conference was subsequently canceled.) At about the same time, Chinese Foreign Minister Chen Yi, who had been sent to Africa to take soundings for the conference, was obliged to report that the neutral nations were unwilling to exclude the Soviet Union and, further, that they would be unwilling to back a formal condemnation of United States policy in Vietnam. Then reaction to Marshal Lin's essay on "People's War" made it clear that non-Communist African leaders were irritated by the suggestion that China considered their anticolonial revolutions to be only preludes to the socialist revolution in which, presumably, they, the present leaders, would disappear. African leaders consider that the achievement of self-government and independence from colonial rule *was* their revolution.

Strong statements have been made in Africa against China. The government of Malawi had to get rid of some Cabinet ministers for allegedly conspiring with the Chinese; Kenya expelled the New China News Agency correspondent "in the interests of national security"; Burundi, once regarded as safely in the Chinese camp, expelled Peking's diplomatic mission.

In Latin America the Chinese have had even less success. And (perhaps the unkindest cut of all), even Fidel Castro, whose rise to power had been hailed in Peking as a demonstration of the validity of the Chinese analysis of the Latin American revolutionary situation, has taken to denouncing China.

While the Chinese proclaim the "true teaching" loudly and frequently, in practice their foreign policy has been one of relative caution and restraint.

Perhaps the most significant example of their caution and restraint is Eastern Asia. Most of the Chinese leaders have never been outside of China, and, with the exception of Chou En-lai, they have had little contact with foreigners.

They see the world's most powerful nation establishing posts along their periphery. They see American bases and garrisons in Korea, in Japan, on Taiwan, in the Philippines, in South Vietnam, and in Thailand. They know our nuclear-armed bombers on Okinawa are aimed at Peking. They know that American ground troops in Vietnam number nearly half a million and they know that we are building up in Thailand. They see the U.S. Seventh Fleet in the Western Pacific and in the Taiwan Straits, the South China Sea, and the Gulf of Tonkin. They see American planes, on bombing missions over North Vietnam, violating Chinese airspace; on at least two occasions the U.S. State Department has acknowledged "accidentally" bombing villages across the border in southern China. They see increasing pressure on North Vietnam which, despite United States protestations to the contrary, may well be a threat to the existence of that country. They see all this; yet there are no Chinese soldiers fighting in Vietnam. No Chinese MIGS fly to protect Hanoi from our bombs.

Why have they acted with such restraint? The Chinese presumably have some fear of United States retaliation. Our generals have been very outspoken in their determination not to put up with a privileged sanctuary or long, drawn-out negotiations as was the case in the Korean War.

Peking's caution is also demonstrated by her toleration of the "imperialist enclaves" of Hong Kong and Macao. While a Chinese decision to move on Hong Kong may well provoke a British response, it is difficult to see how effective such a response could be. Hong Kong is, of course, of great economic value to China, the source of much of her foreign exchange. Further, the Chinese could not be certain that a move against Hong Kong would not provoke an American reaction.

Given the evidence of Chinese failures and caution, the conclusion must be that China is not today a threat to the United States; that if she is bent on fomenting a world-wide revolution, she is not in a position to push very hard; and that, despite her provocative propaganda barrages, China is going to be compelled to devote most of her efforts and resources to her own internal problems.

There remains one longer-range question to be raised, if not answered: namely, the question of whether China and the United States are on a collision course. The likelihood of confrontation, of ultimate showdown, is not immediate, not inevitable. One scholar, Professor Donald Zagoria of Columbia University, has suggested that eventually it may be easier for a Communist China to adjust differences with the United States than with the Soviet Union. He told the Senate Foreign Relations Committee in 1966 that "a recent French emissary in Peking was told that the Americans were, after all, only an enemy, and a respected one, whereas the Russians were traitors and traitors could never be forgiven."

The United States and China need not be on a collision course, but there are elements of danger in the developing situation. These dangers arise because present U. S. policy in the Far East is based largely on unsubstantiated assumptions.

First, we assume that revolutions throughout the less-developed world are a Chinese-inspired wave of the future and that Vietnam is a test case for guerrilla warfare and for wars of national liberation. Constant reiteration of this claim by both sides tends to place the prestige of each on the line. Yet there is no good reason for accepting this characterization of the Vietnam War.

The techniques of the Chinese revolution have not as yet proved fully successful in China; they are a long way from inspiring revolution in other parts of the world.

Second, we continuously assert that the Southeast Asia situation is analogous to previous situations and experiences in Asia and also in Europe. Military containment worked in Europe and in Korea, according to the theory; thus it is the method to be applied in Southeast Asia or in any other test area. But the conditions under which containment was effective in Europe and in Korea do not exist in Southeast Asia, which is marked by deep ethnic and social divisions; by instability, political and social; by deep antagonism to the remnants of Western colonialism; and by the desire for change rather than for a return to the past.

In an unstable and fluid society, such as that in Vietnam, there are usually persons or groups who will cooperate with outside forces or protectors—with Russia, with China, with England, with France, with Japan, with the United States—seeking to hold on to power and privilege or to build new strength and status under protection. Unless such cooperation between the protector and the ruling group is involved in activities which also meet the needs of the people or which promise to do so within a reasonable time, it usually serves to do no more than buy time and postpone the reckoning. War lords are ordinarily not willing to sacrifice their power, nor landlords to accept land reform; neither are those whose power and profits depend on disorder and instability likely to make any great contribution to the "nation building" which our Southeast Asia experts say is our objective and which is fundamental to order in that part of the world.

The question that is calculated to disarm any opposition is "Do you want another Munich?" as though there were any significant points of similarity or even of comparability between Europe prior to World War II and Southeast Asia of the 1960's.

Two other concepts, balance of power, carried over from the nineteenth century, and "filling the power vacuum," an early twentieth-century idea, are also adduced as applicable to our engagement in Southeast Asia. Neither one is applicable. The problem is not one of balance of power in Asia. Even if it were, balance could not be maintained against China with the support we now have from South Vietnam, Thailand, Korea, the Philippines, Australia, and New Zealand. If Asia is to be stabilized by a balance of powers, the great, and potentially great, powers of Asia must themselves be involved: Japan, China, India, and Indonesia.

None of the present instruments of international security in the area is likely to become a real basis for an Asian security system, because they were inspired by non-Asians and have been avoided by the major Asian powers. SEATO, the Southeast Asia Treaty Organization, was constructed on a basis that was unacceptable to the Asians who might make the difference. It has not been effective. Of its members, only Thailand is providing more than token assistance to the United States in Vietnam, and this assistance is largely in the form of base rights. The Philippines has not been willing, despite strong U.S. pressure, to send combat forces. Pakistan is not only opposed to American policy, but has been receiving military assistance from Communist China and refused to attend a meeting of the SEATO Council held in Washington in April 1967.

As for SEATO's non-Asian members, France is outspoken in her opposition to our Vietnam policy, and even Britain goes along with increasing reluctance. Australia and New Zealand, to whom the United States is also bound by the ANZUS Pact, are SEATO members who are making relatively small contributions in Vietnam in the form of troops. But these two countries, for obvious reasons, cannot be expected to be major, important elements in an Asian power balance.

The "vacuum concept" does not apply either, since this assumes that a power which stood against an opposite power has been destroyed or removed. The reality of Southeast Asia is not a complex of nation states but a rather generalized, undifferentiated world of neither pressure nor vacuum.

If balance of power is to be the stabilizing way for Asia, it will be achieved only when the great powers of Asia—Japan, India, and Indonesia—are able to play major roles. Their potential is great.

By any measurement other than land area, Japan is one of the biggest countries in the world. Its Gross National Product is approximately equal to that of the whole of Latin America and is double the size of Africa's. During recent years, Japan's economic growth rate has averaged close to 10 percent, the highest of any major country. Even if the Japanese hold growth rate down to 7½ percent, as they are now attempting to do, they may soon pass Britain, France, and Germany to become the third largest economic unit in the world.

Japan is one of the world's major industrial powers and the only Asian power who can help her neighbors along the difficult road to development. The enormous ingenuity and diligence of the Japanese people, their skill and experience of modernization in an Asian setting, can be of great value. Japan's experience with fertilizers, seed types, and agricultural machinery is perhaps more meaningful for most of Asia than is our own or that of the Russians.

Our former Ambassador to Japan, Edwin O. Reischauer, has said, "There can be little doubt that within five or ten years Japan will be playing a major role, possibly *the* major role in the Far East." Part of the present imbalance in Asia is the result of Japan's disappearance as a power after World War II.

Our relations with Japan and Japan's with the world will soon reach a critical point. Support for military alliance with the United States has diminished in Japan, particularly since the Vietnam War. We will have to consider, therefore, whether the maintenance of the present alliance beyond 1970 will be in the best interest of Japan and of the United States and of order in Asia. We will have to consider whether it might not be wiser to permit Japan the freedom to seek or to provide leadership in Asia on her own. We must anticipate that the Asians in the 1970's or 1980's are no more likely to be satisfied with the protection of an American nuclear umbrella over which they have no control than are the Europeans in the 1960's.

India's difficulties are not so much of a constitutional as of an economic nature and her future role will depend on her ability to meet these problems.

Indonesia is unable to play a major role on the Asian scene at present. Her economy is in a state of ruin, and the most optimistic estimates predict that recovery from the excesses of the Sukarno years will be slow. In addition, the relationship between Java and the other islands of Indonesia raises problems of national unity which work against Indonesia's becoming a major force in the area for many years.

Many of our problems today are the result of our unwillingness or inability in the past to anticipate what might be the shape of the world twenty years in the future. Few Americans expected in 1945 that twenty years later we would still have 225,000 troops in Europe. We have 55,000 troops in South Korea fourteen years after the end of the fighting; yet, at the height of the Korean conflict we never had as many troops committed as we have in Vietnam. We must ask whether the United States is prepared to maintain from 100,000 to 200,000 troops in South Vietnam as well, for fifteen or twenty years after the fighting stops. If we are not prepared to do so, the process must be reversed before temporary commitment assumes the character of a permanent establishment and an irritation in the changed context of another generation. We must begin now the adjustments of attitude which will be necessary if we are to reduce or liquidate our commitments in Asia.

There is never a totally painless way to pull back from either unwise, ill-advised, or outdated ideas or commitments. But throughout history, mighty nations have learned the limits of power. There are lessons to be learned from Athens, from Rome, from sixteenth-century Spain, and from England and France in this century.

A nation has prestige according to its merits. America's contribution to world civilization must be more than a continuous performance demonstration that we can police the planet.

Index

Acheson, Dean, 25-29, 30, 31, 33, 35; quoted, 27
Adenauer, Konrad, 124
Africa, 125-32; Acheson policy on, 29; arms supplied to, 41, 42, 44, 48-49, 61; China and, 174; Dulles and, 31; U.S. exploitation of, 130
Agency for International Development (AID), 52
aircraft: supplied to Middle East, 42-44, 66; supplied to Latin America, 45, 58-59
Algeria, 44, 119, 129, 152
Alliance for Progress, 42, 97, 104, 108, 111-12
American Revolution, 31, 100
Angola, 129-30
ANZUS treaty. See Australia, New Zealand, United States Security Pact
Arbenz, Jacobo, 33, 75, 103
Argentina, 45, 59, 98
arms: sale of, 41-42; financial practices, 63-64; Germany and, 64-65; promotion of, 47-48, 51-53, 63, 64-66; U.S., 39-41, 65-66
Arms Control and Disarmament Agency, U.S., 51-52, 66

Asia: arms supplied to, 41, 42, 53; revolt of, 131; U.S. and, 29, 139, 180, 181. See also names of countries, e.g., China
atomic bomb, 150, 154. See also nuclear weapons
atomic energy, international control of, 28
Australia, 164, 178, 179
Australia, New Zealand, United States Security Pact (ANZUS), 29, 42, 179

Baghdad Pact, 31, 55. See also Central Treaty Organization
balance of payments, 48, 59-60, 64
balance of power, concept of, 178-79
Ball, George, 121
Bantu peoples, 127
Batista, Juan, 78
Bay of Pigs. See Cuba, proposed invasion of
Bolivia, 61
bombing, civilian, 150, 152
Brazil, 45, 46, 58
Bretton Woods Agreement, 28
Britain: Africa and, 127, 130; arms sales, 41, 43, 45, 47,

59; China and, 176; House of Commons, 75; SEATO and, 151, 178-79; U.S. and, 40, 132

Buchan, Alastair, quoted, 50-51

Burke, Edmund, quoted, 118

Burma, 73-74, 172

Burundi, 130, 174

Cambodia, 172

Canada, 112, 123, 164

Caroline Islands, 139

Castro, Fidel, 72, 104, 110, 175

Central Intelligence Agency (CIA), 32-33, 35, 71-93

Central Treaty Organization (CENTO), 20, 42, 55

Chad, Republic of, 127

Chen Yi, 174

Chiang Kai-shek, 20, 34

Chile, 45, 97, 110-11

China, 157-77; CIA and, 72, 74; civilization, 158-61; Communist, 20, 31-32, 46, 53, 72, 161-67, 169; foreign policy, 167, 172-73; India and, 168, 169-70, 173-74; Nationalist, 73-74, 161, 171; Pakistan and, 178; Soviet Union and, 41; U.S. policy on, 19, 31-32, 34, 55, 59, 61, 110, 150, 157-58, 176-77. See also Taiwan

Chou En-lai, 175

Churchill, Winston, 25

civic action programs, 56-58

cold war, 28, 39, 81, 86, 118

Colombia, 101, 112

colonialism, 99, 127-29, 145, 177

Commager, Henry Steele, 87; quoted, 87-88, 131-32

communism: alleged, in Dominican Republic, 21, 105, 106; alleged, in Guatemala, 75; Asian, 173-74; Chinese, 159, 160-61, 172-73; CIA and, 88; Dulles, John Foster, on, 29-30; European, 117; Latin American, 57, 100, 110-11; U.S. policy to contain, 20, 28, 32, 46-47, 55-56, 60-61

Congo, 129-30; Belgian, 128, 131

Congress, U.S., 25; Acheson and, 26-27, 28, 30; CIA and, 32-33, 71, 80, 89-93; Dulles, John Foster, and, 31; Micronesia and, 140, 144; military assistance and, 45, 47, 48, 62, 67, 118-19; resolutions by, 27, 31, 32, 34; Rusk and, 34, 35; sugar quotas, 107. See also House; Senate

counterinsurgency, U.S. theory of, 56

Cuba: military assistance to, 49; proposed invasion of, 21, 32-33, 35, 72-73, 78-82, 104; U.S. base in, 102

Defense, U.S. Department of, 35, 42-43, 49, 52, 53; and arms control, 65-66; and arms industry, 41-42, 48, 50-52, 62-65; counterinsurgency theory, 56; Germany and, 64-65; Latin America and, 59; Micronesia and, 145; Vietnam and, 50

deGaulle, Charles, 117, 119, 120-21

developing countries, 48, 53, 60, 65, 107, 112

diplomacy: principles of, 27; Rusk on, 34

disarmament, 19; Geneva conference on, 66

disease, evidence of in Micronesia, 141

Dominican Republic, 21, 97, 101, 104-8, 113

Dulles, Allen, 29-30, 32-33, 82

Dulles, John Foster, 20, 26, 29-33, 34, 35, 55, 82, 103, 119; quoted, 30-32

Egypt. See United Arab Republic

Eisenhower, Dwight David, 26, 34, 62, 76-77, 78, 79, 133; administration of, 32, 103

Eisenhower Doctrine, 20

enclave policy, proposed, 154

England. See Britain

Erhard, Ludwig, 65

escalation, military, 152, 154

Ethiopia, 42, 44, 48, 127, 129, 168, 171

Europe, U.S. relations with, 83, 117-24, 180-81

European Defense Community, 32, 118-19

European Economic Cooperation, Organization for, 111

Export-Import Bank, 63-64

FAO. See United Nations Food and Agriculture Organization

Fontaine, André, quoted, 120-21

Foreign Affairs, 83, 97

foreign aid, economic, 97-98, 103-4

Foreign Assistance Act, 51

foreign policy, U.S., 19-21, 25, 39; Acheson concept of, 29; arms sales and, 52, 53, 59; CIA and, 32-33, 71, 80, 90-91; Defense Department and, 50; Dulles concept of,

20, 29-30; on Africa, 130-32; on China, 157-58, 168-72; on Latin America, 99, 102-6, 112-13; on Micronesia, 144-45; Secretaries of State and, 25-35; Senate and, 90

Formosa, 31. See also Taiwan

France, 119-20; Africa and, 127-28, 130; arms exported by, 41, 43; NATO and, 25, 117, 121, 123; SEATO and, 179; U.S. and, 32, 35, 40, 117, 120-21, 151

Frei, Eduardo, quoted, 97, 110-11

Fulbright, J. William, 93; quoted, 80

Galbraith, J. Kenneth, 46

Gavin, James M., 154

Germany, 117, 130; Federal Republic of, 45, 64-65, 117, 118, 124; rearmament of, 118, 124; Truman-Acheson policy toward, 28; U.S. and, 120

Ghana, 130

Good Neighbor Policy, 102

Gordon, Lincoln, 46

grant aid, military, 42, 45, 48, 49-50

grants, academic, 52-53

"great arc theory," 55-56

Great Leap Forward, 163

Greece, U.S. aid to, 26, 28, 42, 61

Guam, 139, 143

Guatemala, 33, 58, 75, 79, 103

Guinea, 49

Haiti, 49, 98, 101, 104

Hawaii, 139, 143

Herter, Christian, 77

Hickenlooper, Bourke, 93
Hilsman, Roger, 74; quoted, 35, 76, 78
Hitler, Adolf, 168
Ho Chi Minh, 173
Honduras, 58, 104
Hong Kong, 168, 176
House of Representatives, U.S.: Appropriations Committee, 47, 92-93, Armed Services Committee, 92; Foreign Affairs Committee, 59; military assistance and, 119
Hungary, 32

imperialism, Western, 130, 161
India, 178, 179, 180; arms supplied to, 46-47; China and, 168, 169-70, 173
Indochina, French, 119
Indonesia, 55, 76, 173, 178, 179, 180
Inner Ring, dangers of, 86
Intelligence Operations, proposed Congressional Committee on, 90-93
inter-American force, proposed, 109
Inter-American Treaty of Reciprocal Assistance, 103
interest rates, international, 64
International Bank for Reconstruction and Development, 28
Irán: CIA and, 75; military aid to, 42, 43-44, 61, 66
Iraq, 42, 43
Islam, 127, 128
Israel, 43, 132-35
Italy, 171
Ivory Coast, 130

Jackson, Henry, 34

Jamaica, 49
Japan, 178-80; China and, 161, 166, 168, 174; language, 159; Micronesia and, 139; treaties with, 29, 31; U.S. and, 19, 139, 178, 180
Johnson, Lyndon B., 26, 34, 66, 88, 97, 109, 123, 133, 139; quoted, 122
Jordan, Kingdom of, 42, 43

Kennan, George, 152-53
Kennedy, John F., 26, 33-34, 72-73, 74, 76, 79-80, 104, 133
Kenya, 44, 128, 174
Khrushchev, Nikita, 72, 78
Korea: Chinese aggression in, 168-69; language, 159; North, 41, 174; South, 42, 61; U.S. and, 31, 139, 151, 175, 177, 178, 180
Korean War, 20, 27, 28-29, 72, 169, 176, 181
Kuss, Henry, 63; quoted, 47-48, 59
Kwajalein atoll, 145
Laos, 33, 50, 74-75, 82
Latin America, 95-114; China and, 175; civic action programs in, 56-58; military assistance to, 41, 42, 45, 49, 50, 56-59; proposed resolution on, 35; treaties with, 20. See also aircraft; Alliance for Progress; Monroe Doctrine; and names of countries, e.g., Argentina
League of Nations, 19, 130
Lebanon, 20-21, 32
Lee Kuan Yew, 75, 60
Lend-Lease Program, 28, 40, Lenin, V. I., 160, 161
Leopold II, king of Belgium, 128

Lewis, C. S., quoted, 86

Liberia, 49

Libya, 42

Lieuwen, Edwin, quoted, 56-57

Lin Piao, 168

literacy, Latin American, 98, 106

Lleras Restrepo, Carlos, quoted, 142

loans, international, 63-64

McNamara, Robert, 46, 48, 54, 62; quoted, 53-54, 55, 59

Macao, 168, 176

Malawi, 174

Mali, 49, 127

Manchuria, 168, 169

Mann, Thomas, 105

Mansfield, Mike, 89, 93; quoted, 62

Mao Tse-tung, 165-67, 173

Mariana Islands, 139

Marines, U.S., 101

Marshall, George C., 26, 33, 140

Marshall Islands, 139

Marshall Plan, 20, 28, 111, 117

Mauritania, 127, 129

Mexico, 102

Michigan State University, 83

Micronesia, 139-45

Middle East, 132-35; Africa and, 127; arms supplied to, 41, 42, 44, 67; Joint Resolution on, 31-32; U.S. commitments in, 29. See also names of countries, e.g., Iran

militarism, Latin American, 57, 58, 106

military advisers, U.S., 52, 61

Military Assistance Program, U.S., 39-40, 42, 45, 46, 48, 50-51; civic action and, 58; critics of, 62; defense industry and, 63; foreign policy and, 53-55, 58-60; goals of, 60, 61-62; Latin America and, 103; profits and, 62; training under, 53

military bases, U.S., 42, 102, 139, 143, 175

missiles, 43, 143, 145

Monroe Doctrine, 19, 31, 99-100

Monroe, James, quoted, 99-100

Moorehead, Alan, 142

Morgenthau, Henry, 26

Morocco, 44, 129

Mossadegh, Mohammed, 33, 75

most-favored-nation policy, 19

Mozambique, 130

Multilateral Force, proposed European, 34, 120

Mussolini, Benito, 168

Mutual Defense Assistance Act, 40

Mutual Security Act, 19

napalm, 152

Nasser, Gamal Abdel, 31, 43, 174

national liberation, wars of, 100, 177

National Liberation Front, 83, 154

National Security Act, 81

National Security Council, 71-72, 77, 84

National Student Association, CIA and, 84, 88

nationalism, Chinese, 161, 166, 168, 172

Nehru, Jawaharlal, 170

New Zealand, 178, 179

Ngo Dinh Diem, 83

Nicaragua, 58, 101
Niger, Republic of, 127
Nigeria, 127, 128
North Africa, 127, 131. See also names of countries, e.g., Algeria
North Atlantic Treaty Organization (NATO), 117-18, 120-24; Dulles and, 31, 32; France and, 25; Rusk and, 35; U.S. and, 20, 40, 42, 50, 130
nuclear weapons, 61, 122, 180; control of, 124; proposed multilateral force, 120; proposed treaty on, 34; test ban, 34, 174

Okinawa, 139, 175
open-door policy, 19
opium, smuggling of, 73
Organization of American States (OAS), 103, 105-6, 112; proposed reform of, 109, 111
Outer Space, Treaty on, 34-35

Pacific Islands, U.S. Trust Territory of, see Micronesia
pacification, 152, 154
Pakistan, 46-47, 151, 173, 178-79
Panama, Republic of, 101
Panama Canal, 100-101
Paraguay, 58
Peace Corps, Micronesia and, 141-42
Pearson, L. B., quoted, 123
Peru, 45, 58, 61, 104
Philippines, 42, 76, 139, 175, 178
Phoumi, Nosavan, 74
Platt Amendment, 101-2
Podgorny, Nikolai, 171
Poland, 29
Portugal, 42, 128, 130

power vacuum, concept of, 178, 179
Puerto Rico, 144
Punta del Este, conference at, 98

Quemoy and Matsu, 32, 168

Ramparts magazine, 83
Ranstead, Donald D., quoted, 46
Reischauer, Edwin O., quoted, 180
Rhodesia, 130
rice production, 172
Rio Treaty, 103, 105
Rome, ancient, 153-54, 181
Roosevelt, Franklin D., 25, 26, 133; quoted, 102
Roosevelt, Theodore, 101
Rusk, Dean, 26, 33-35, 75, 151
Russia. See Soviet Union
Rwanda, 129

San Francisco Conference on World Organization, 29
Saudi Arabia, 42, 43
Schlesinger, Arthur, Jr., 74; quoted, 29-30, 82
Senate, U.S.: Appropriations and Armed Services committees, 89, 92; CIA and, 80, 89; Foreign Relations Committee, 35, 41, 46, 49-50, 51-52, 53-54, 59, 60, 66, 67, 77, 87, 90-91, 93, 121, 140, 142, 152-53, 157, 176; Government Operations Committee, 34; military assistance and, 62
Singapore, 75
Somali peoples, 127, 128-29
Somalia, 44, 129
Sorensen, Theodore, quoted, 79

South Africa, 127, 130
Southeast Asia. *See* Burma, Laos, Thailand, Vietnam
Southeast Asia Treaty Organization (SEATO), 31, 42, 46, 55, 151, 178-79
Souvanna Phouma, Prince, 75
Soviet Union: aims of, 117; arms exported by, 41, 43, 44; China and, 41, 164, 166, 169, 171, 173-74; Hungarian revolt against, 32; U.S. and, 28, 40, 53, 55-56, 59, 61-62, 67, 76-77, 78, 110, 120, 123, 144; Vietnam and, 177
Spain, 42, 181
Spanish American War, 19
Stalin, Josef, 25, 72, 160, 166
State, U.S. Department of: Acheson and, 28; arms sales and, 41-42, 47, 51; China and, 175; CIA and, 74, 78, 82, 84; France and, 120; Latin America and, 45-46; Rusk and, 33, 35, 75
submarine warfare, 150
Sudan, 49
Suez crisis, 32, 134
sugar industry, 107, 113
Sukarno, Achmed, 76, 180
Sun Yat-sen, 161
Syria, 43

Taiwan, 34, 42, 151, 168, 175. *See also* Formosa
tariff regulations, 112, 144-45
Tashkent Agreement, 47, 174
technical assistance, U.S., 83
Test Ban Treaty, 34, 174
Thailand, 50, 139, 172, 178
Tibet, 168, 169, 170-71
Tonkin Gulf Resolution, 35, 151
tourism, potential, in Micronesia, 145

Toynbee, Arnold, quoted, 153-54
trade relations, U.S.-Latin American, 106-7, 112-13
treaty obligations, U.S., 20; Acheson on, 26; Dulles on, 20, 31, 32; Rusk on, 34-35; Vietnam and, 151. *See also* Central Treaty Organization, North Atlantic Treaty Organization
Trujillo, Rafael, 108
Truman, Harry S., 26, 29, 31, 80-81, 132; quoted, 80-81
Truman Doctrine, 26, 28
Turkey, U.S. aid to, 26, 28, 42

U-2 reconnaissance flights, 72, 76-77
Uganda, 127
United Arab Republic, 43, 55, 127, 174
United Kingdom. *See* Britain
United Nations: Africa and, 130, 131; Acheson and, 28; Burma and, 73-74; Dulles and, 20, 29, 30; Korea and, 169; Latin America and, 110; Outer Space Treaty and, 34-35; trusteeships, 139-41, 143-44; U.S. and, 20, 132, 135; Vietnam and, 154
United Nations Food and Agriculture Organization, 28
United Nations Relief and Rehabilitation Administration, 28
United States Information Agency (USIA), 57
United States of America. *See* arms, sale of; Central Intelligence Agency; Congress;

Defense, Department of; foreign policy; Military Assistance Program; State, Department of
United States of Europe, proposed, 119-20
U.S. Seventh Fleet, 168, 175
Upper Volta, 130
Uruguay, 98

Venezuela, 45, 49
Versailles Peace Conference, 29
Viet Cong, 83
Vietnam, 149-54, 173, 177-78; Africa and, 174; China and, 171-72, 175; CIA and, 33, 83, 85; language, 159; military bases, 139, 175; military assistance to, 50, 54-55, 178-79, 181; North,

bombing of, 85, 175; Rusk and, 34, 35; U.S. objectives in, 149-51; war in, 35, 45, 54-55, 142, 177, 178, 180
Vorys, John, quoted, 119

Warsaw Pact nations, 124
wheat, imported by China, 164, 172
Wilson, Woodrow, 29, 101
Wood, General Robert, quoted, 47
World Health Organization, 141
World War I, 19, 149-50
World War II, 19-20, 28-29, 39-40, 117, 133, 139, 149-50, 152, 168, 173

Zagoria, Donald, quoted, 176

41 weeks on the Best Seller List!

CAPABLE
OF
HONOR

ALLEN DRURY

Now $1.25

Walter Dobius was the most powerful columnist in the nation and with the right turn of a phrase he could either make or break a senator, a governor, perhaps even . . .

But no, that was impossible. This was America, a democracy; that sort of thing just couldn't happen here. Or could it?

"Allen Drury has written another terrific political novel . . . hurdles you into the middle of Washington's big-time intrigue with the same exciting style of writing that gained literary fame for his Pulitzer Prize-winning ADVISE AND CONSENT. . . . breathless reading." —*Tampa Tribune*

"Outstanding" —*Fort Wayne News-Sentinel*

A DELL BOOK

The #1 bestseller that dazzled the nation

MADAME SARAH

CORNELIA OTIS SKINNER
95c

On stage she was the greatest actress the
world has ever known. Off stage she was
a woman who made her own rules for life
and love. Passionate, willful, breathtaking,
maddening, and wonderful, she reigned
supreme over a glamorous and glorious
age. Her name—
SARAH BERNHARDT

"One of the most beautiful of human stories."
— *New York Times Book Review*

"Dramatic . . . tempestuous . . . scintillating . . .
this book is a 'must'."
— *Los Angeles Times*

"Racy . . . romantic . . . memorable."
— *Life Magazine*

A DELL BOOK

If you cannot obtain copies of this title at your local bookstore, just send
the price (plus 10c per copy for handling and postage) to Dell Books, Box
2291, Grand Central Post Office, New York, N.Y. 10017. No postage or
handling charge is required on any order of five or more books.